RELAXING THERAPY

COLORING BOOK

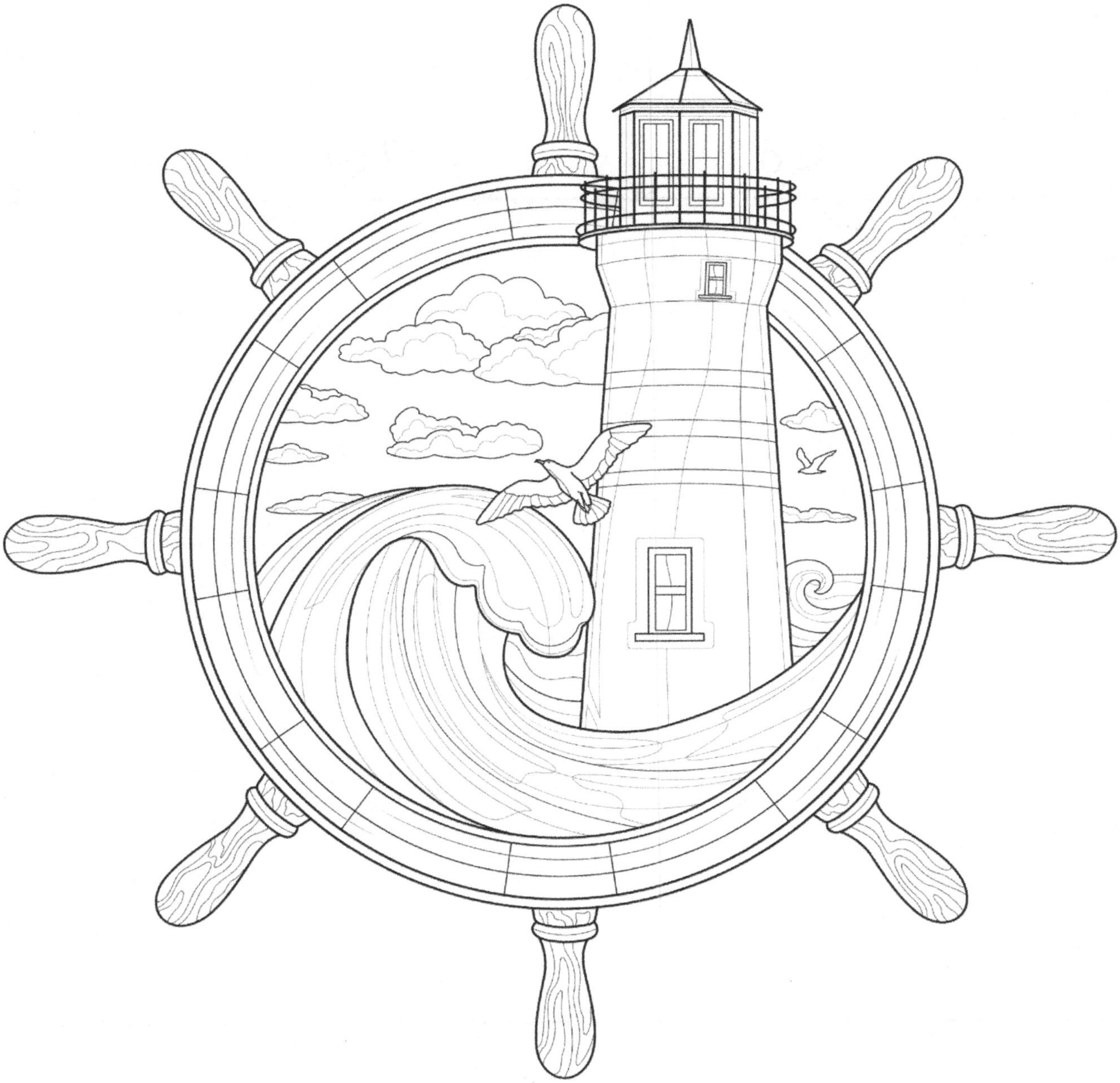

This Book

Belongs to

_____

This book is published by Therapy Seminary Publishers.

Printed in the U.S.A

First Edition: 2023

ISBN: **978-1-961902-14-5**

DISCLAIMER: The contents of this book, including but not limited to its text, graphics, images, and other material are for informational purposes only. The Content is not intended to be a substitute for professional medical advice, diagnosis, or treatment. Always seek the advice of your physician or other qualified health provider with any questions you may have regarding a medical condition. Never disregard professional medical advice or delay in seeking it because of something you have read in this book.

CONTENTS

TEST COLOR PAGE

SELF-HEALING

In moments of uncertainty, reaffirm to yourself consistently:

"Harmony prevails; all is well.
Every event is unfolding for my ultimate benefit.
From this circumstance, only positivity will arise.
I am secure and protected."

This mantra, when held close, can act as a transformative force in your life.

INTRODUCTION

In the bustling world of constant notifications, never-ending to-do lists, and accelerating demands, we often find ourselves in need of a haven. A sanctuary where time seems to slow down, our breathing matches the rhythm of calm, and our minds find peace. For many, the act of coloring serves as this serene escape.

I fondly recall my grandmother, a radiant woman with a contagiously calm demeanor. Despite the burdens of age and life, she had a unique way of making peace seem almost tangible. Her secret sanctuary? A worn-out sketchbook and a box of crayons.

As a child, I often found her seated at the old mahogany table, her silver hair catching the afternoon sunlight as she hunched over her sketchbook. She colored with a patient grace, her wrinkled fingers guiding the crayon as though it was a wand of tranquility, transforming the stark whiteness of the page into a vibrant mosaic of calm.

Through her, I discovered the Therapeutic Power of Coloring. It was more than a hobby. It was a form of meditation, a silent dialogue between her mind and the paper, transforming anxiety and stress into vivid colors and patterns. Each stroke was a release, each filled space a testament to her tranquility.

Today, science supports this personal anecdote. Studies have shown that coloring can act as an effective relaxation technique, reducing anxiety and promoting mindfulness. It immerses our minds into a state of flow, shifting our focus from our worries to the present moment, the page in front of us, and the colors we choose.

Which brings us to the *Mindfulness Aspect of Coloring*. Mindfulness is about being present in the moment, fully engaged with whatever we are doing without distraction or judgment. It's about observing our thoughts and feelings without being swept up in them. Coloring can help us cultivate this mindfulness.

As we navigate the labyrinth of lines and patterns on a coloring page, we anchor our minds to the act of coloring. We focus on the sensation of the crayon in our hand, the texture of the paper under our fingers, and the vibrant spectrum of colors in front of us. We are mindful of each decision, each color selection, each stroke. This mindful engagement with the present moment fosters our inner tranquility.

In this book, you're not just buying a collection of coloring pages. You're embarking on a journey of relaxation, mindfulness, and inner peace. It's a journey that my grandmother embarked on years ago with a sketchbook and crayons, and now, I'm passing it on to you.

Welcome to your sanctuary, your haven of calm and color. Let's start this therapeutic journey together.

Preparing for Relaxation

Embarking on our therapeutic coloring journey calls for the perfect setting, tools, and mindset. Think of this preparation as a prelude to a spa session, where each element is crafted to serve relaxation on a silver platter.

Creating Your Relaxing Coloring Environment

You are a painter, and your mission is to create a tableau of serenity for your coloring journey. This tranquil haven should be filled with elements that call forth relaxation, allowing your mind to disentangle itself from the cobwebs of thoughts and fully surrender to the rhythmic dance of coloring.

Identify a silent corner in your home that is free from the clatter of the world, where stillness reigns. This could be a cozy chair with a window's view, a soft patch of grass under a tree in your garden, or even a designated area in your room. Illuminate your space with gentle, warm light, enough to caress the pages without glaring into your eyes. Ambient sounds, such as the melody of a soft piano or the gentle whispers of nature, can amplify the tranquility of your environment.

Personalize your space with elements that soothe your soul. It could be a candle that emits a soft, comforting fragrance, or a cherished memento that inspires joy. This is your sanctuary, a realm where you can disconnect from external disturbances and sink into the serene depths of coloring.

Choosing Your Coloring Tools with Awareness

The selection of your coloring tools is a meaningful ritual. It's an intimate moment where you align your artistic arsenal with your emotional landscape. Consider colored pencils for precision, crayons for their nostalgic grip, markers for vibrant strokes, or watercolor pens for a gentle blend of colors. The texture, grip, and color palette of your tools contribute to your unique coloring journey. Trust your intuition to guide you to the tools that feel right, that stir a tingling anticipation at the thought of their colors breathing life into the pages.

Approaching the Coloring Pages

Now, as the stage is set and the tools are at your disposal, you are ready to confront your canvas—the coloring pages. If the intricate designs or the multitude of colors intimidate you, remember, this is not a competition but a personal exploration.

Consider each coloring page as a field of possibilities, ready to bloom under the touch of your colors. Let your instincts pilot your color choices and hand movements. Begin anywhere— from the center spiraling outwards, from the corners converging inwards, or oscillating between large and small designs. There's no script to follow— only the symphony of colors flowing from your heart to the page.

Breathe in the tranquility and breathe out any tension as you color. Each stroke is a ribbon of calm unfurling across the page, each filled contour a declaration of your inner peace.

In the next chapter, we'll delve into the nuances of relaxing coloring techniques. For now, revel in this preparation stage. Soak in the tingling anticipation of the journey that lies ahead. Your passage to the serene world of coloring therapy is open. Let the voyage begin.

Relaxation Affirmations

"Blending Your Artistry with Calming Thoughts"

Picture this - you're seated comfortably, your coloring tools at your disposal, and the "Relaxing Therapy Coloring Book" is opened to a new, intricate design begging for color. Here's where the magic unfolds, where your color palette meets powerful words, and the blend takes you on an extraordinary journey. This voyage not only renders beautiful artwork but also nurtures a tranquil, more relaxed version of yourself.

Visualize each stroke of color not just as a part of the image, but as an echo of calming thoughts reverberating through your mind. Imagine a wave of soothing energy emanating from your fingers, flowing through the pencil and seeping onto the paper. The colors permeate the page, just as a sense of calm pervades your mind.

Unlocking the Strength of Positive Affirmations

Positive affirmations are your personal rays of sunshine, penetrating the grey clouds of anxiety to bathe your mind in warmth and light. These powerful phrases can serve as your armor against anxious thoughts, helping to remodel your mental environment.

Picture yourself working on a complex pattern, feeling a tad anxious about any possible mistakes. Here's where you hit the pause button. Close your eyes and gently affirm, "I am enveloped in peace. My worth is not measured by my mistakes." Let this belief guide your hands as you resume coloring. The perfection of lines or purity of colors becomes insignificant, overshadowed by the peace these affirmations bring.

Crafting Your Coloring Journey with Relaxation Affirmations

As you flip open the next Pages of this book, you'll discover a selection of handpicked relaxation affirmations accompanying each mesmerizing design. Every affirmation is a vital ingredient in the recipe for deep relaxation.

Let's consider an affirmation like, ***"I am serene, I am in the moment."*** As you fill the page with color, chant these words to yourself, syncing their rhythm with the dance of your coloring tool on the paper. Let these words plant seeds in your mind, growing into a vibrant tree of tranquility that outshines your anxieties.

After each coloring session, give yourself a moment of reflection. Ponder on the affirmation, the soothing journey it guided you through, and how it harmonized with your emotions. Absorb its calming influence, let it resonate in your consciousness, and strengthen your inner peace.

The ***"Relaxing Therapy Coloring Book"*** is not just a symphony of colors, but also a melody of words. Each pattern you color and each affirmation you whisper brings you closer to building a peaceful oasis within, a place where anxiety is a stranger. So, keep coloring, keep affirming, and keep nurturing this tranquil inner sanctuary.

All The Best

Therapy Coloring

Relaxing Therapy

I AM
AT PEACE
WITH MYSELF
AND THE
WORLD
AROUND ME.

✷ RELAXING THERAPY COLORING ✷

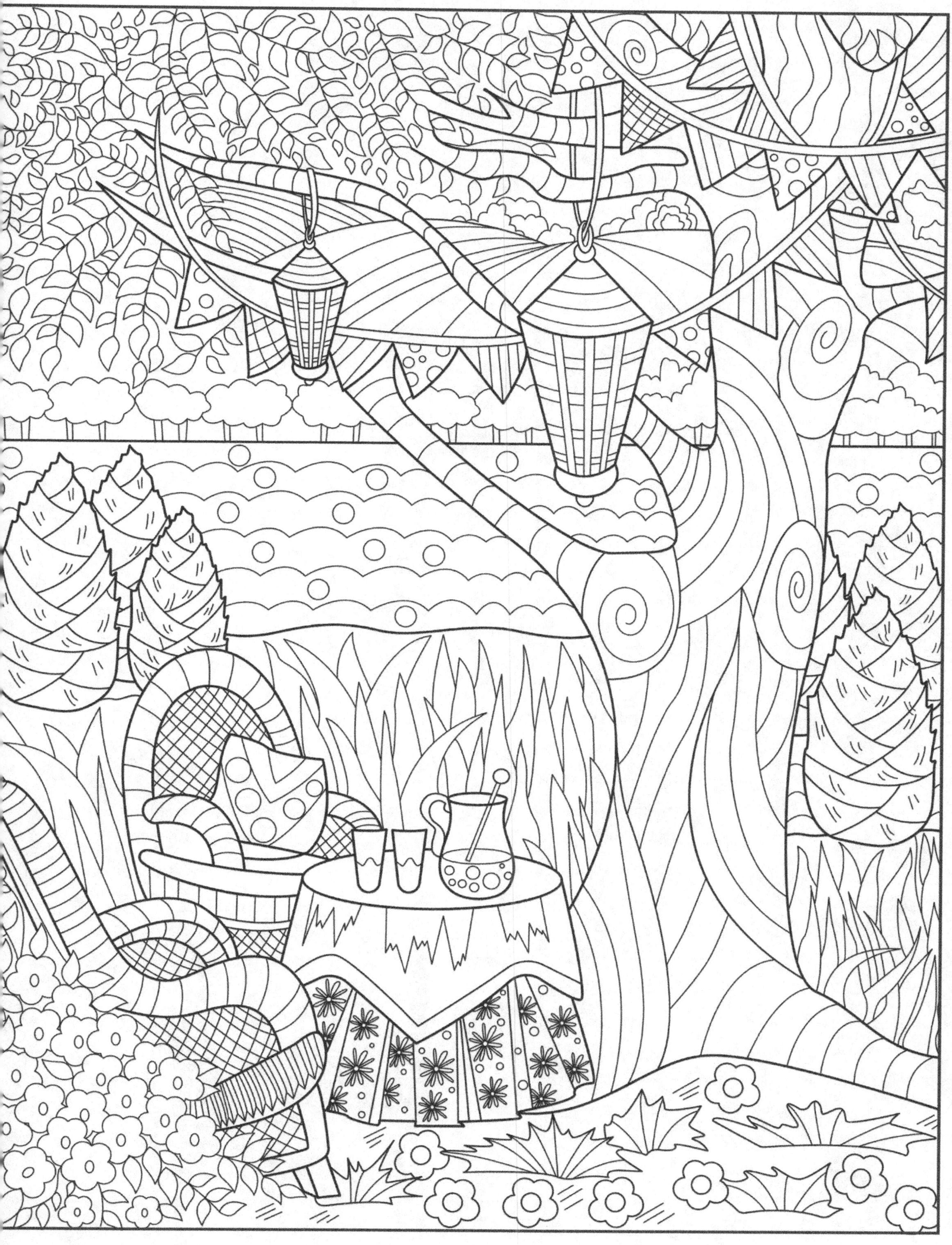

I AM
IN CONTROL
OF MY
BREATH AND
MY
THOUGHTS.

✳ RELAXING THERAPY COLORING ✳

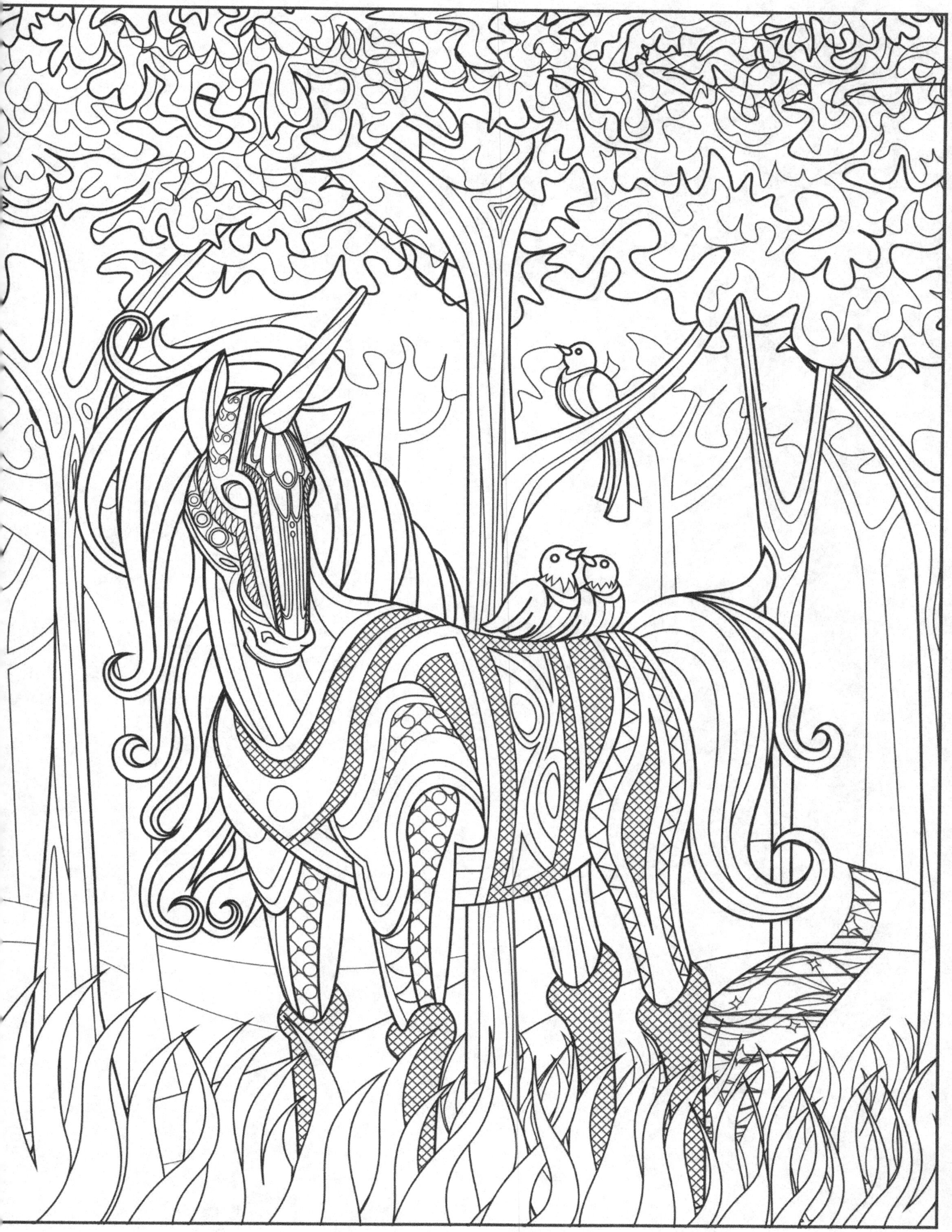

EVERY BREATH I TAKE FILLS ME WITH CALM AND TRANQUILITY.

RELAXING THERAPY COLORING

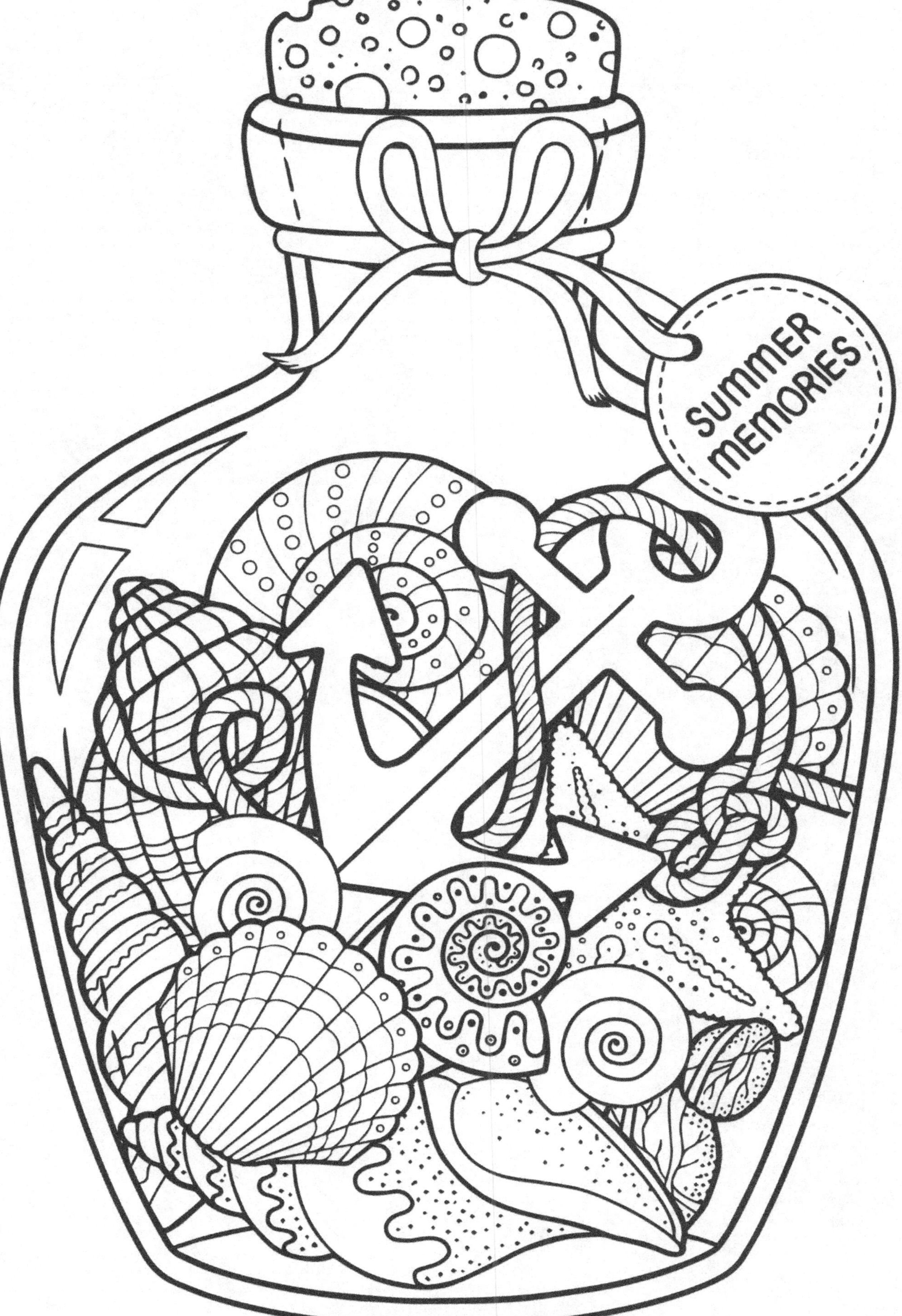
SUMMER
MEMORIES

I AM
PRESENT IN
THIS MOMENT
AND FIND IT
RELAXING.

✶ RELAXING THERAPY COLORING ✶

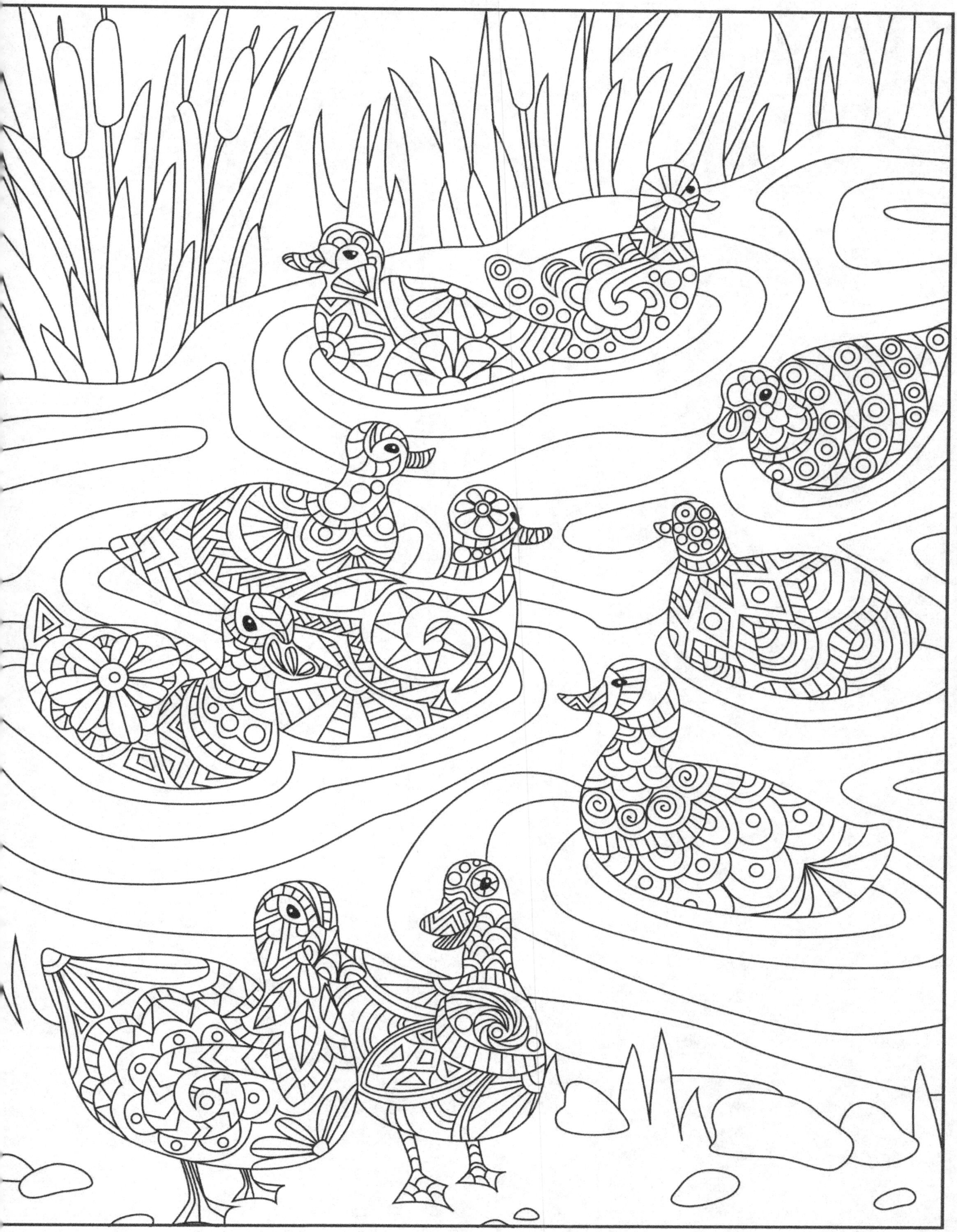

I AM ENVELOPED IN SERENITY AND IT COMFORTS ME.

RELAXING THERAPY COLORING

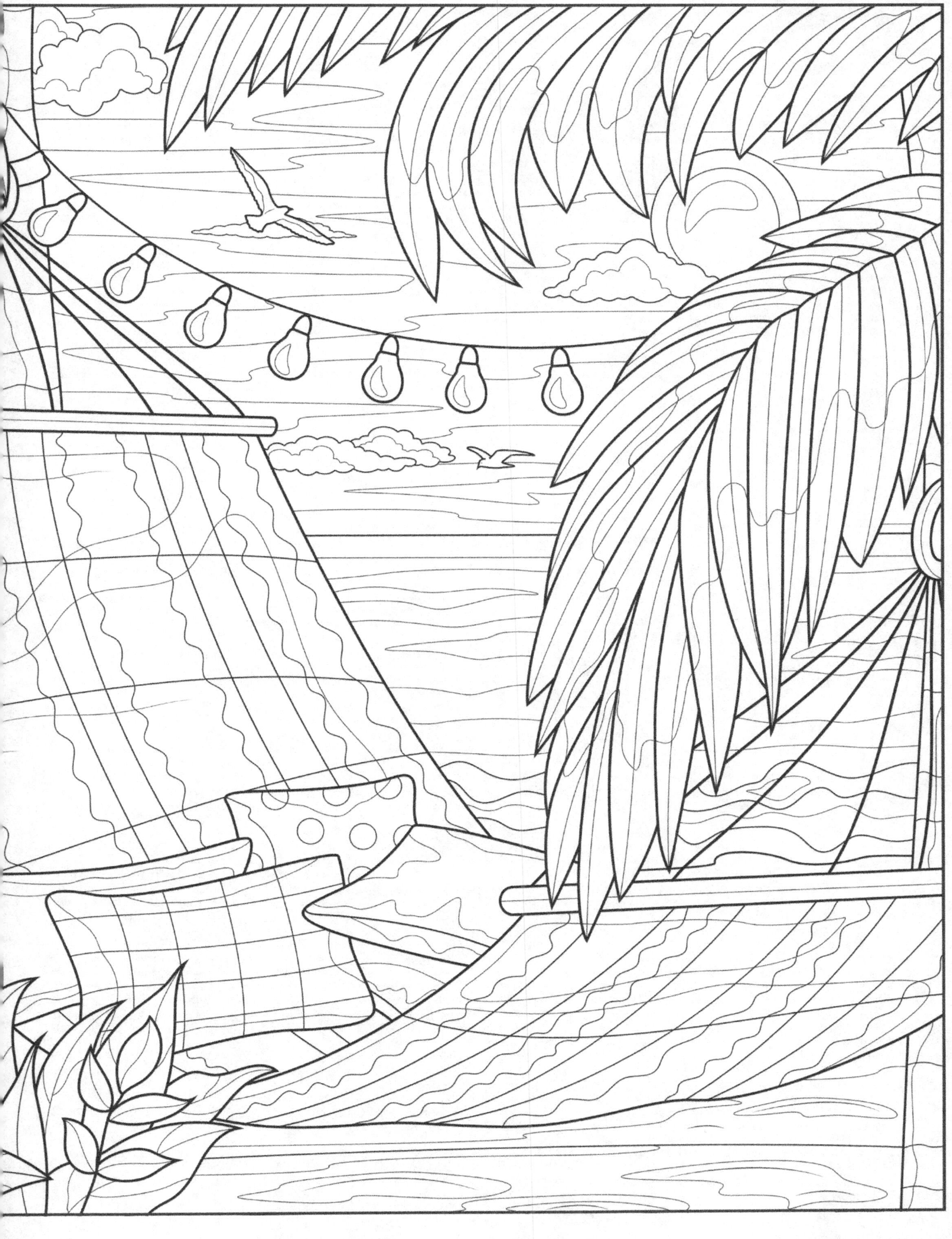

I AM
FREE FROM
WORRY
AND FILLED
WITH
PEACE.

✷ RELAXING THERAPY COLORING ✷

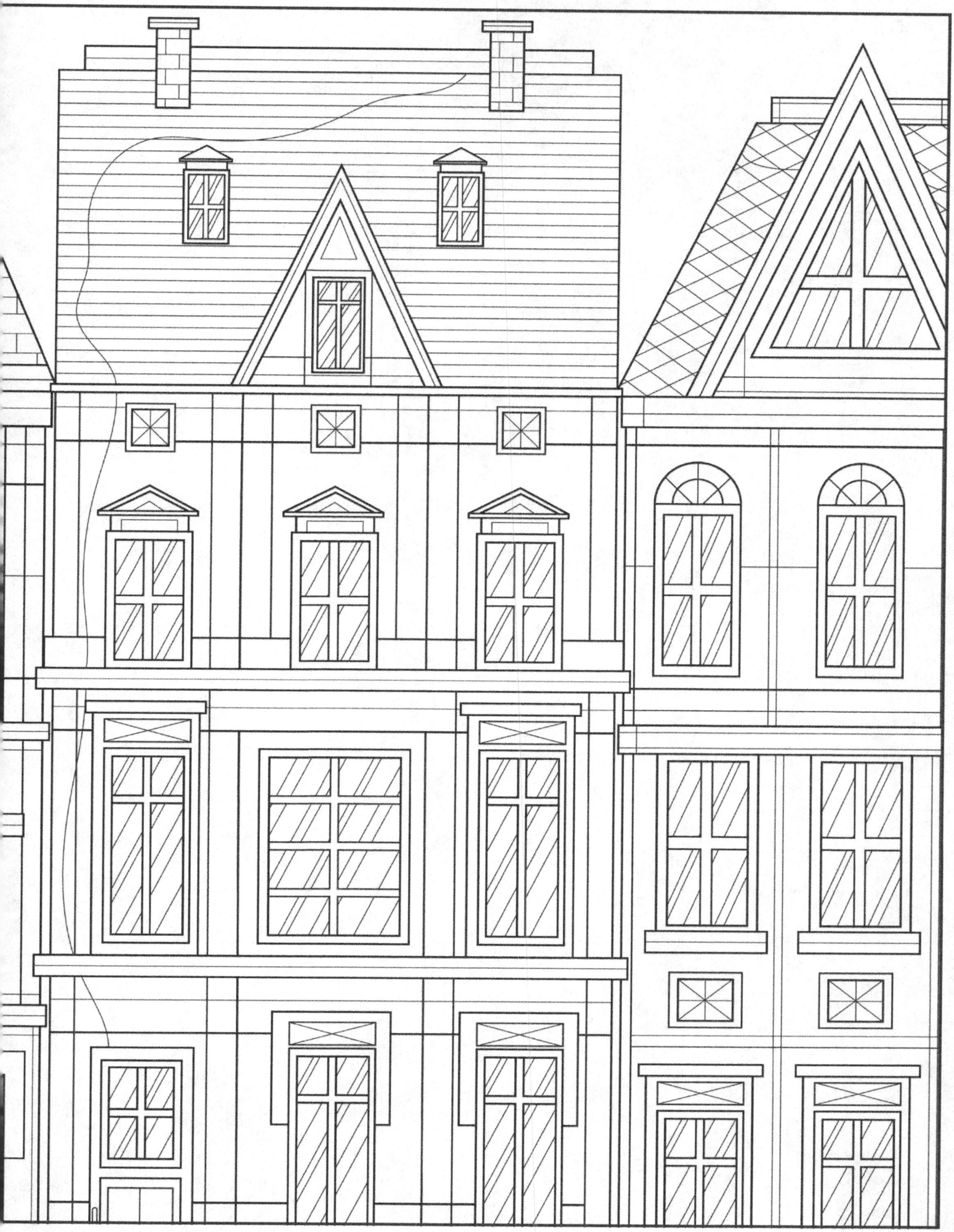

I RADIATE CALM ENERGY AND ATTRACT PEACE.

✶ RELAXING THERAPY COLORING ✶

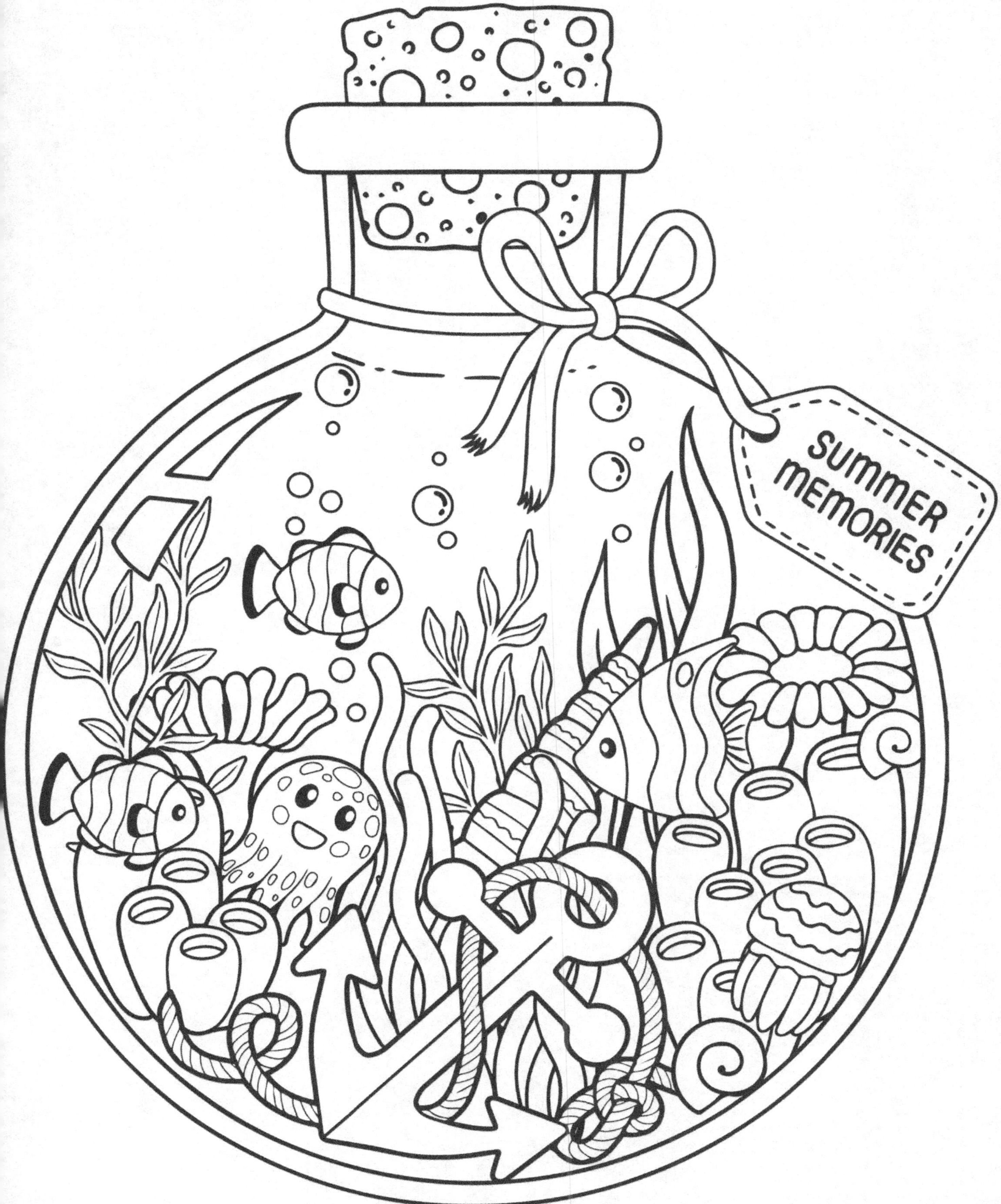
SUMMER
MEMORIES

MY MIND
IS CALM
AND MY
BODY IS
RELAXED.

✷ RELAXING THERAPY COLORING ✷

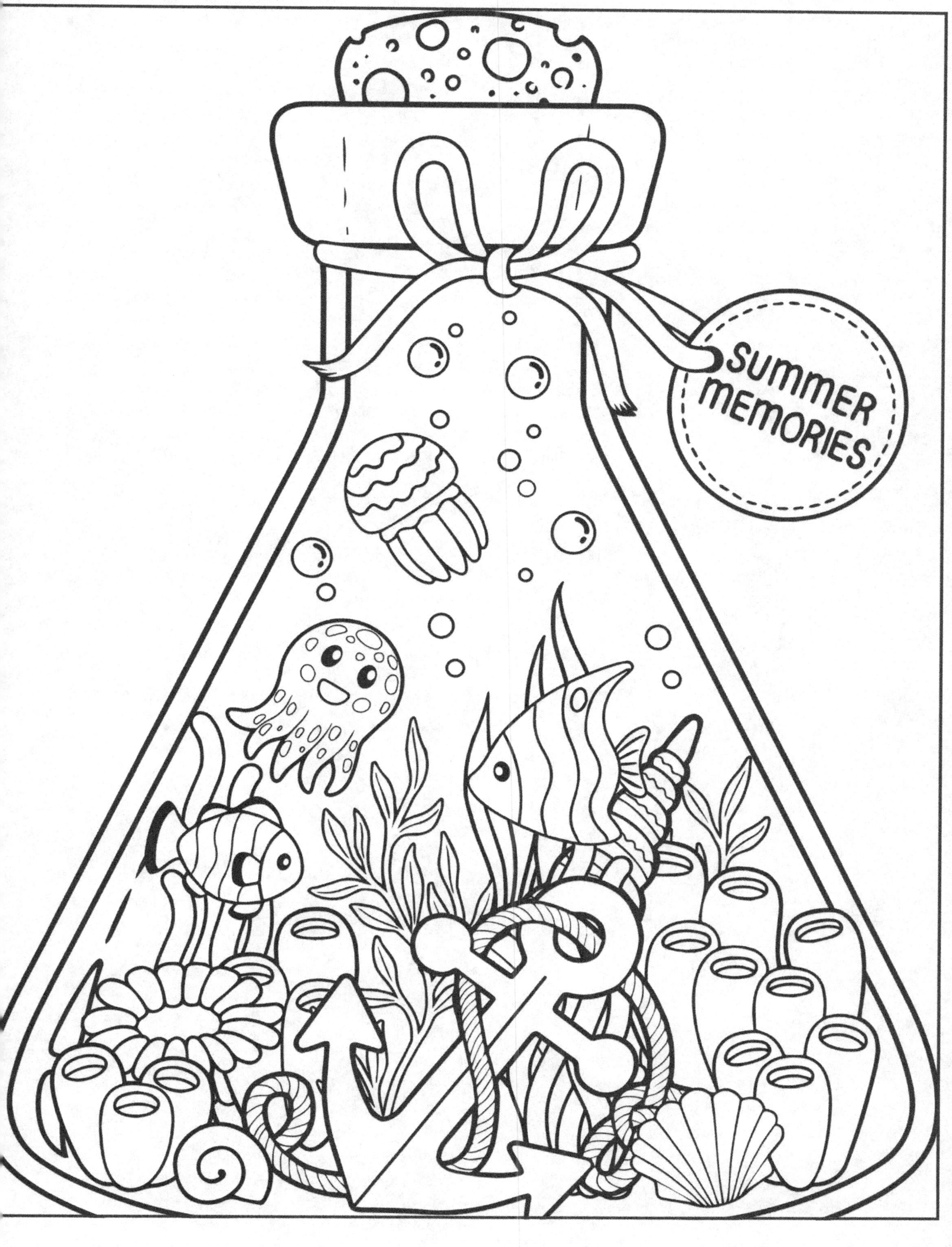
SUMMER
MEMORIES

I RELEASE TENSION WITH EACH EXHALE.

RELAXING THERAPY COLORING

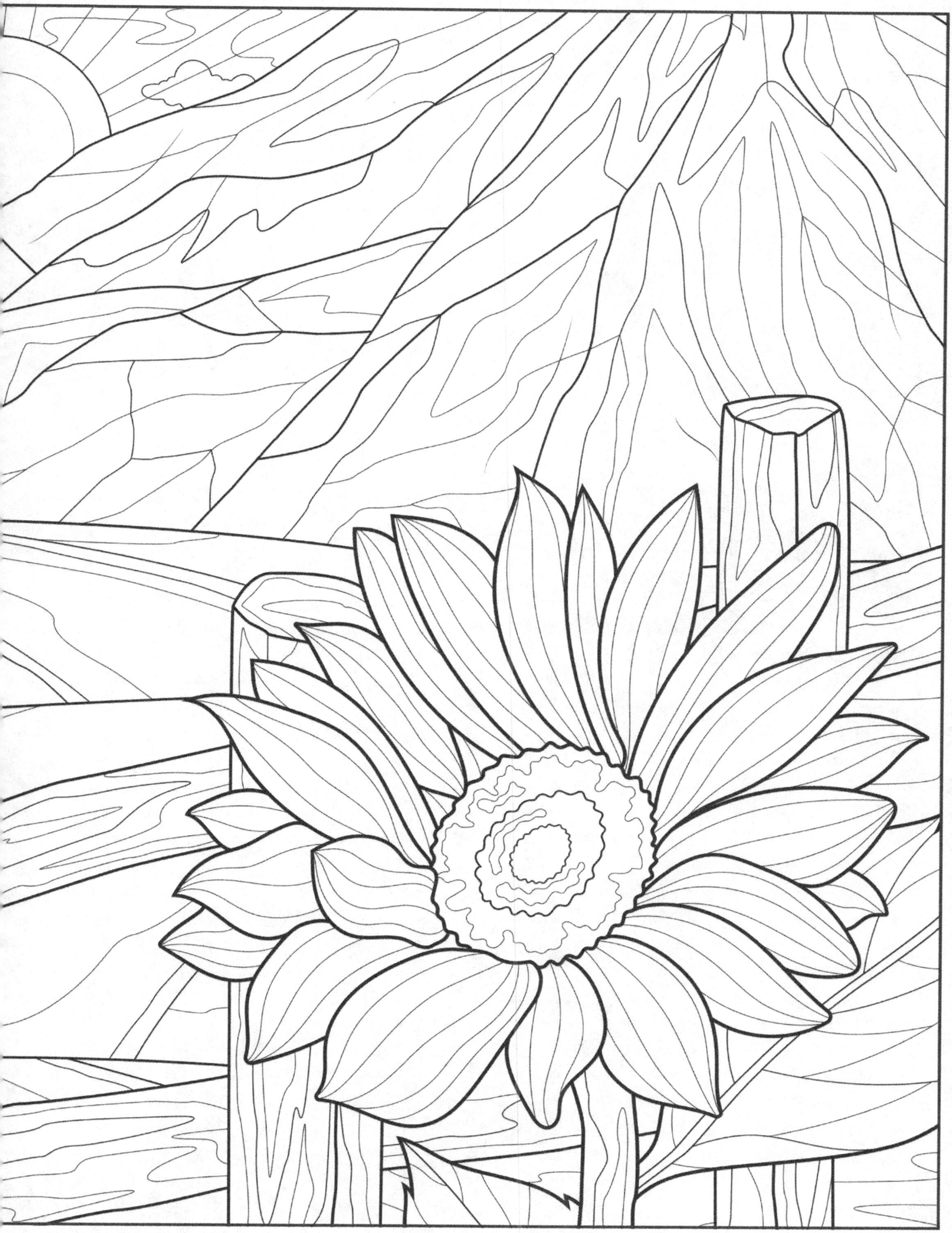

I AM
NAVIGATING
THROUGH
LIFE'S WAVES
WITH EASE
AND GRACE.

✷ RELAXING THERAPY COLORING ✷

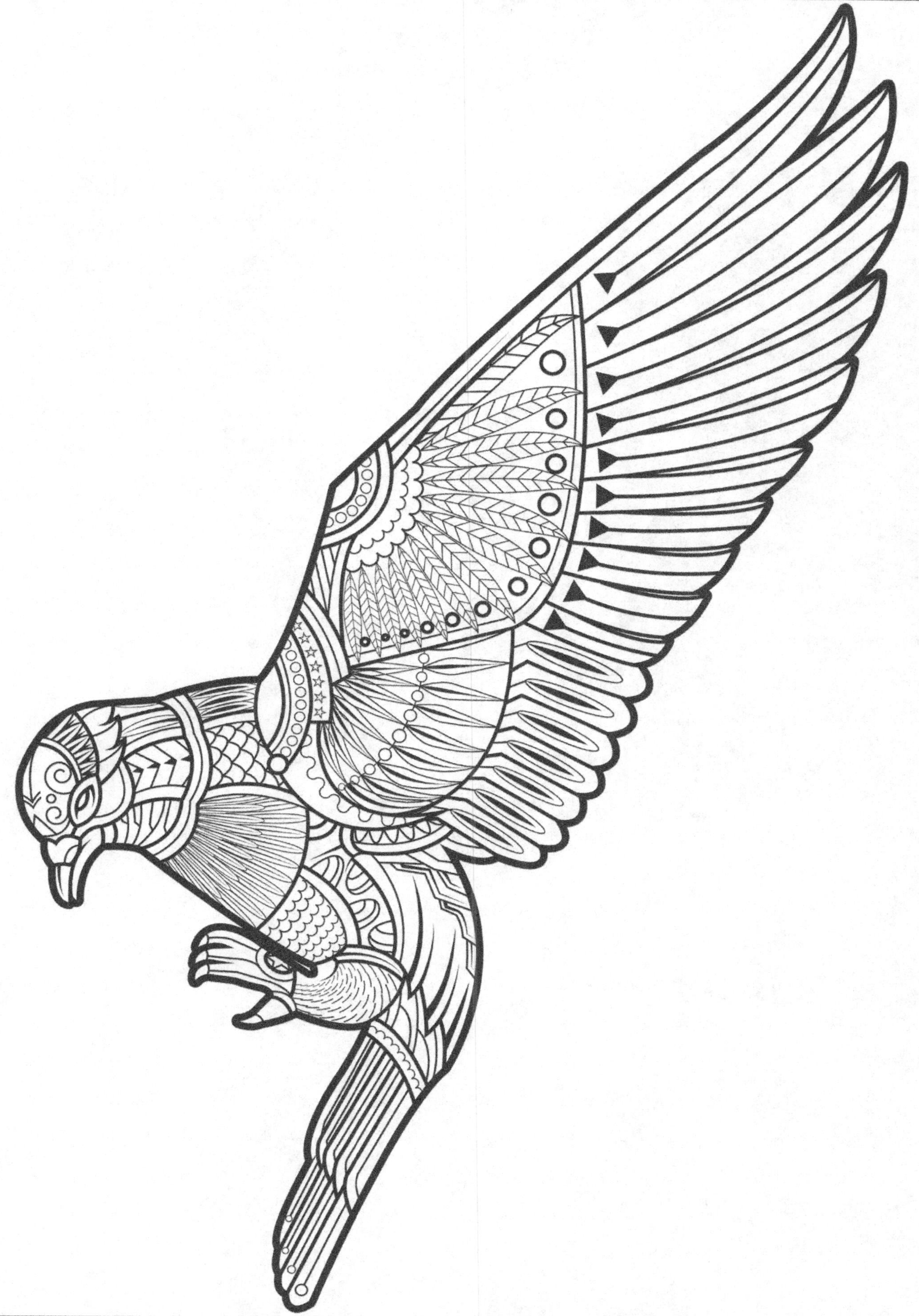

I AM
LETTING GO
OF STRESS
AND
EMBRACING
TRANQUILITY.

✷ RELAXING THERAPY COLORING ✷

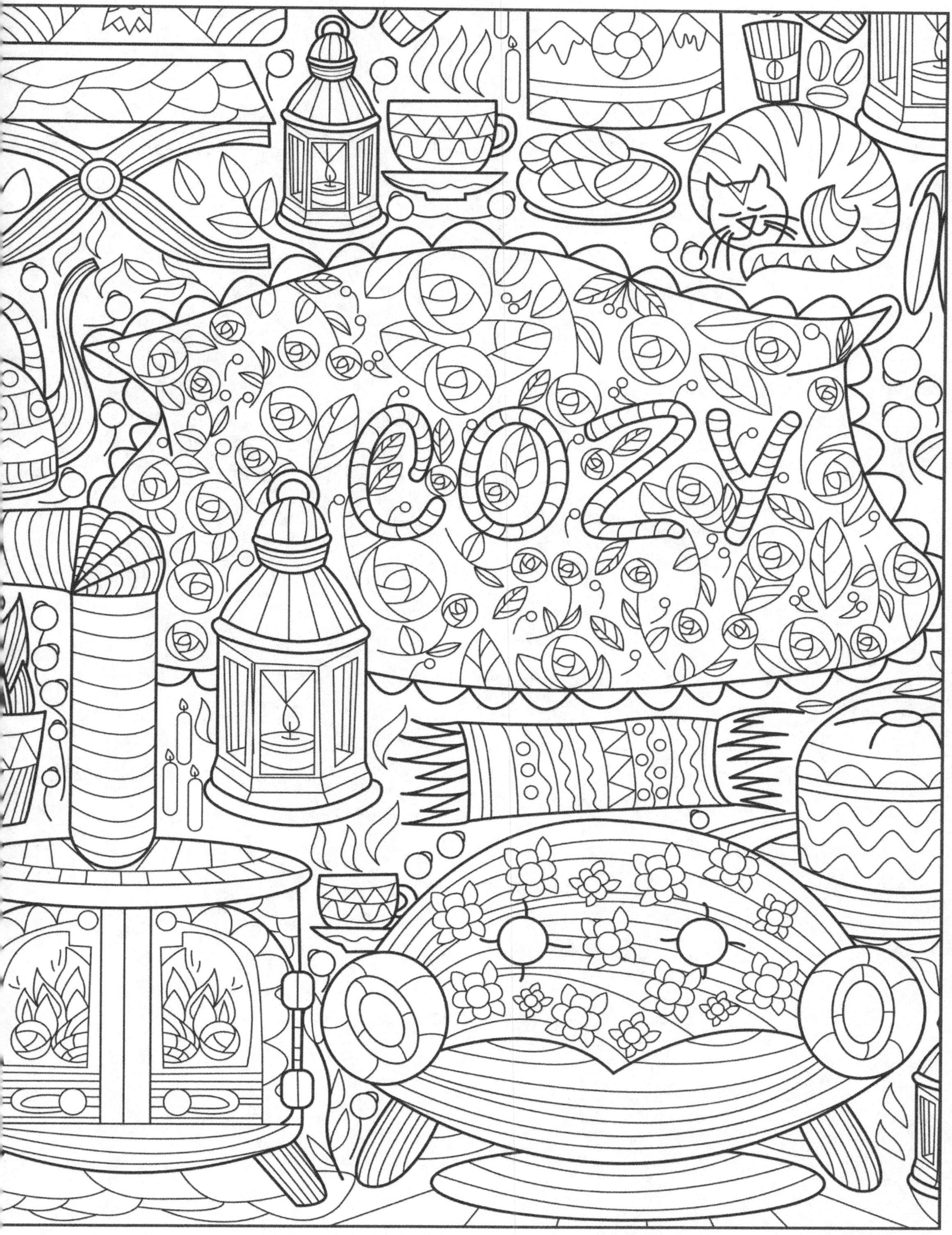
COZY

I AM
BATHING IN
THE LIGHT
OF PEACE
AND
RELAXATION.

✳ RELAXING THERAPY COLORING ✳

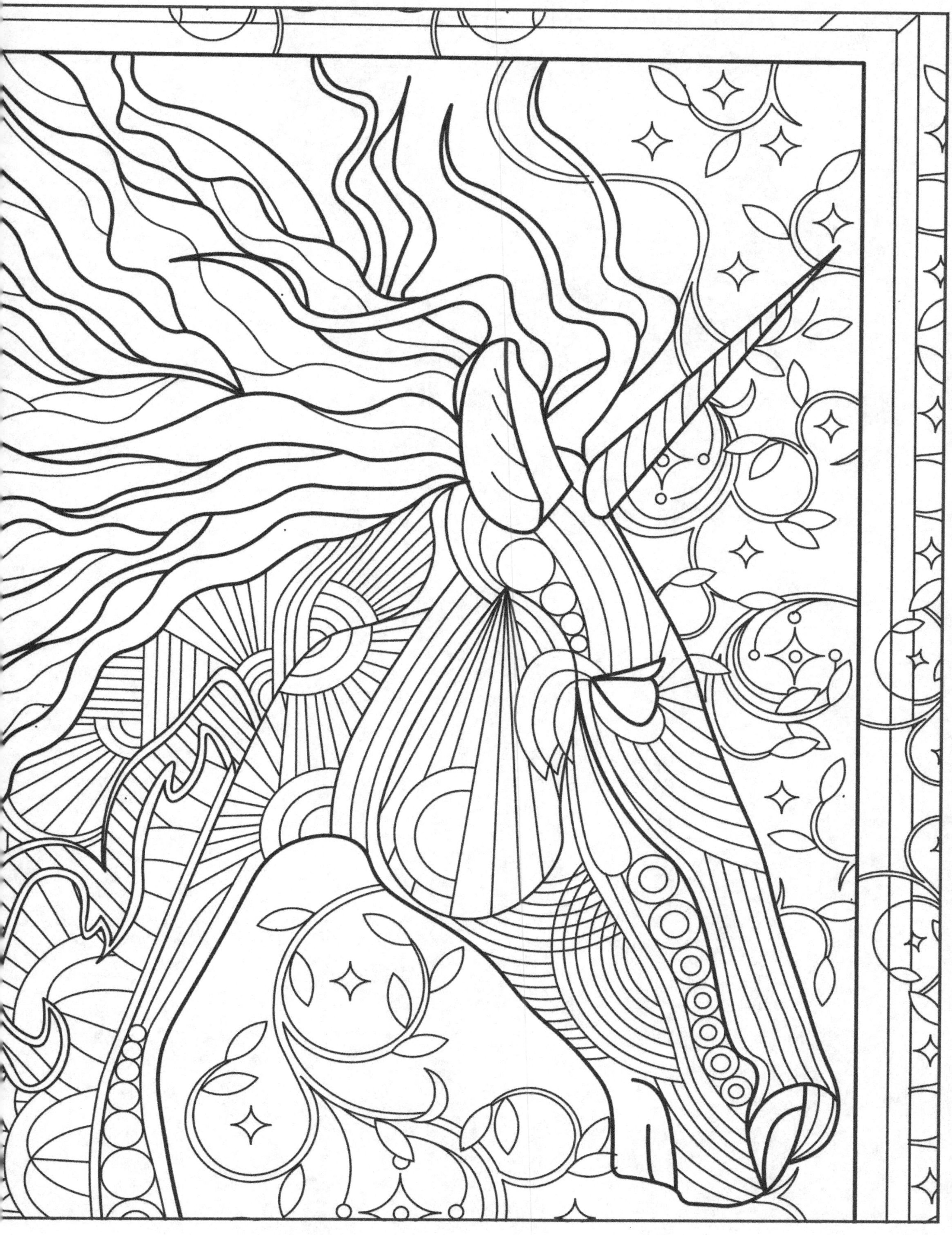

MY MIND
IS SERENE,
JUST LIKE A
STILL LAKE.

✶ RELAXING THERAPY COLORING ✶

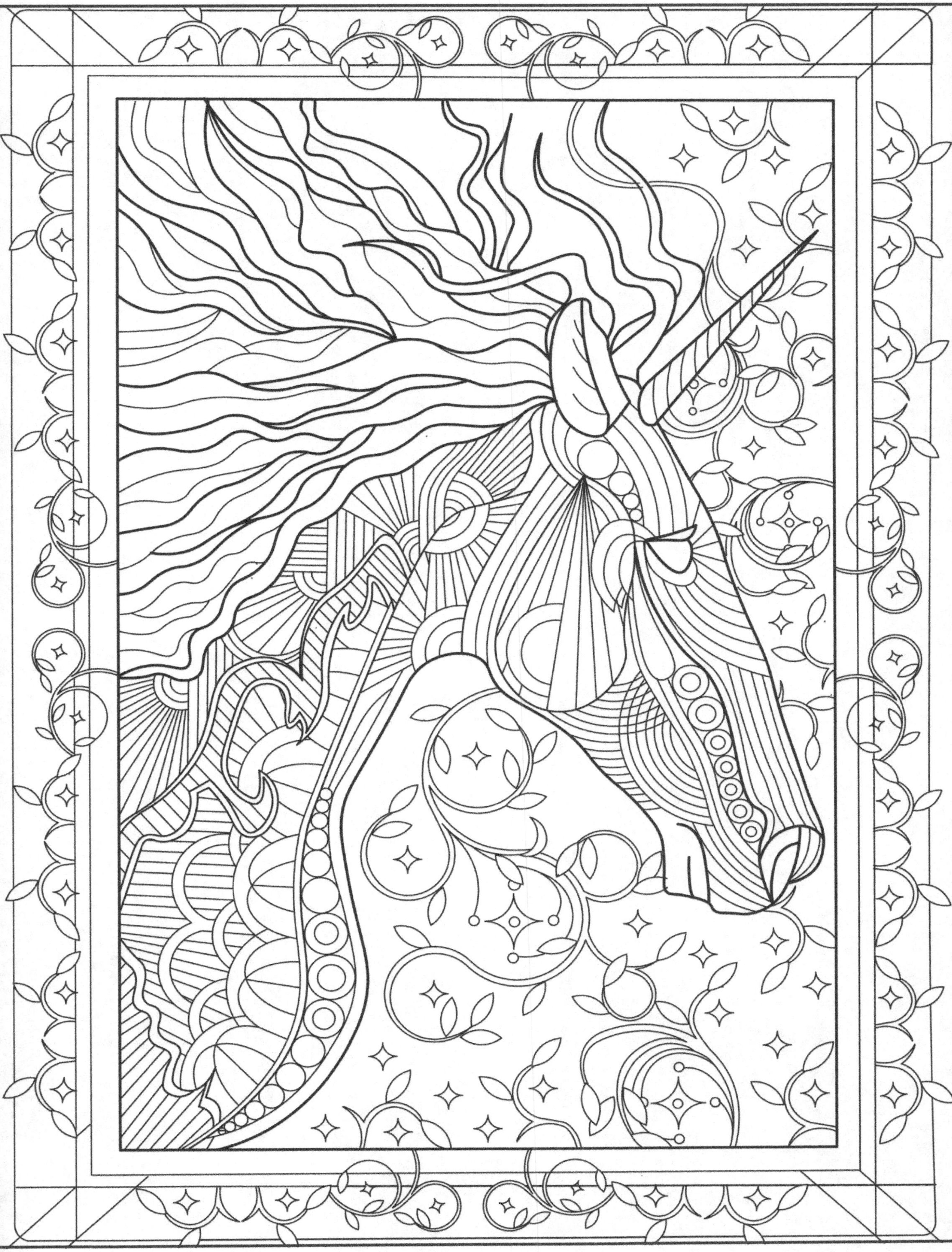

I AM
SAFE,
I AM CALM,
I AM AT
PEACE.

✳ RELAXING THERAPY COLORING ✳

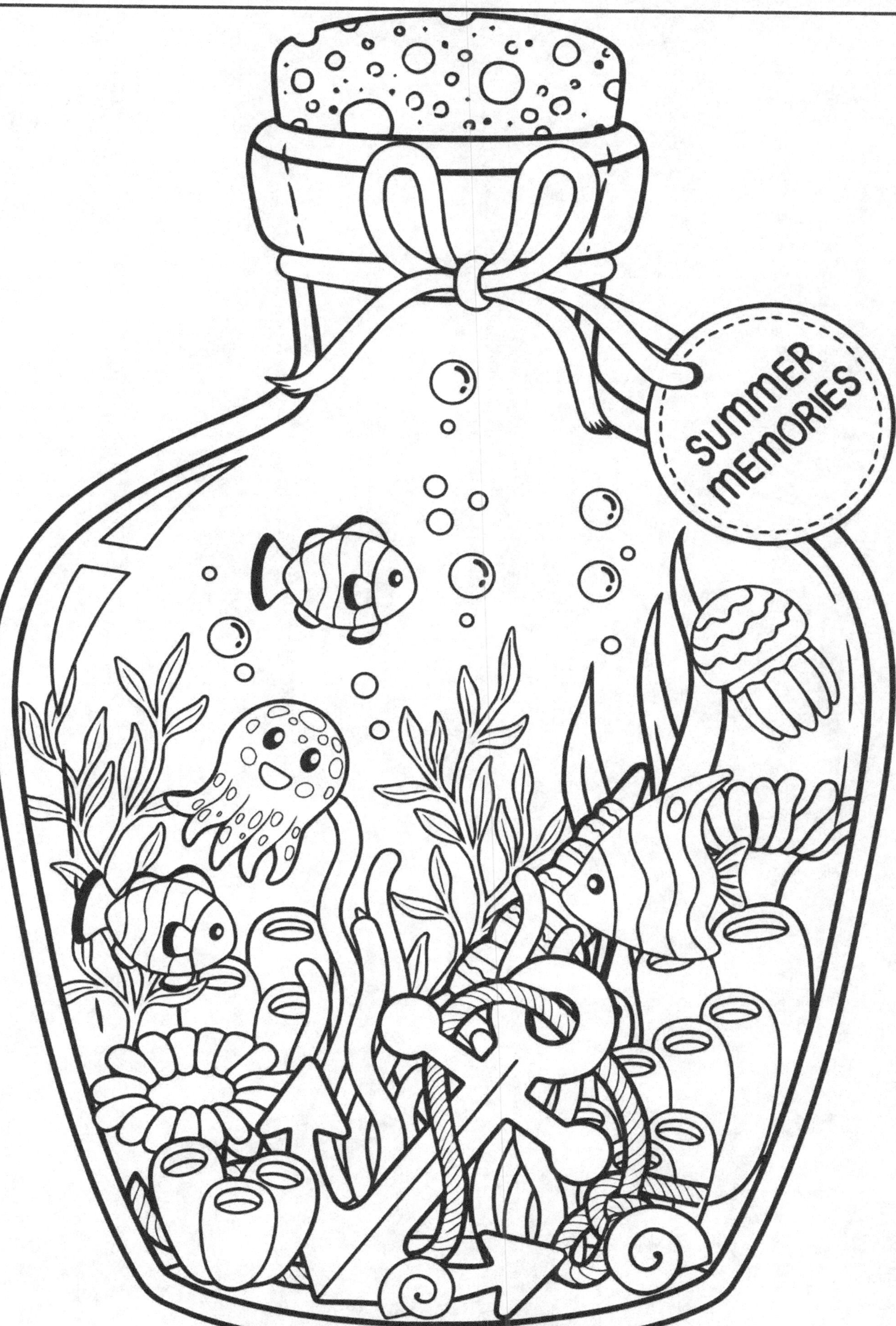
SUMMER
MEMORIES

WITH EACH
BREATH,
I INVITE
TRANQUILITY
INTO
MY LIFE.

RELAXING THERAPY COLORING

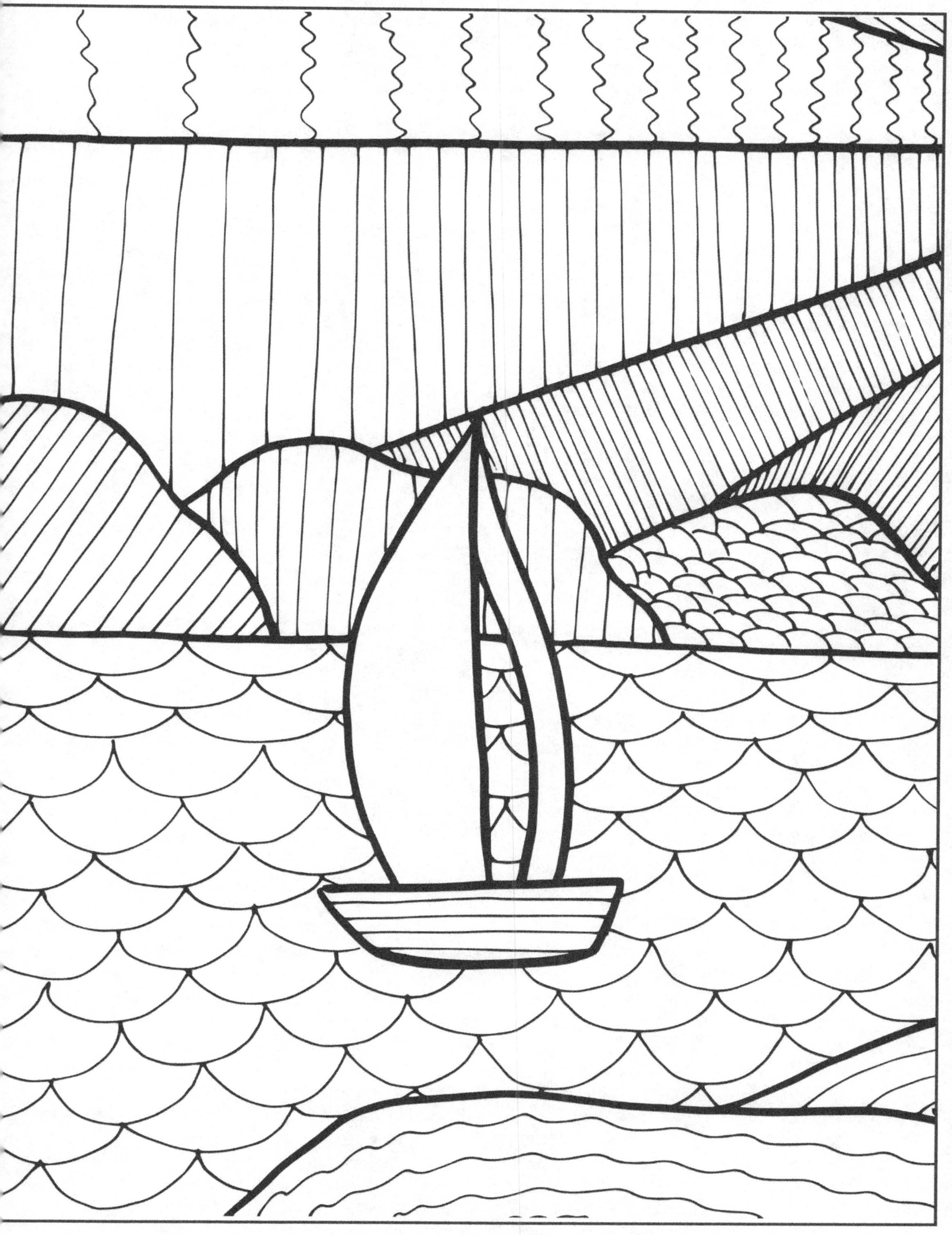

I AM
IN THE
REALM OF
PEACE AND
CALM.

✳ RELAXING THERAPY COLORING ✳

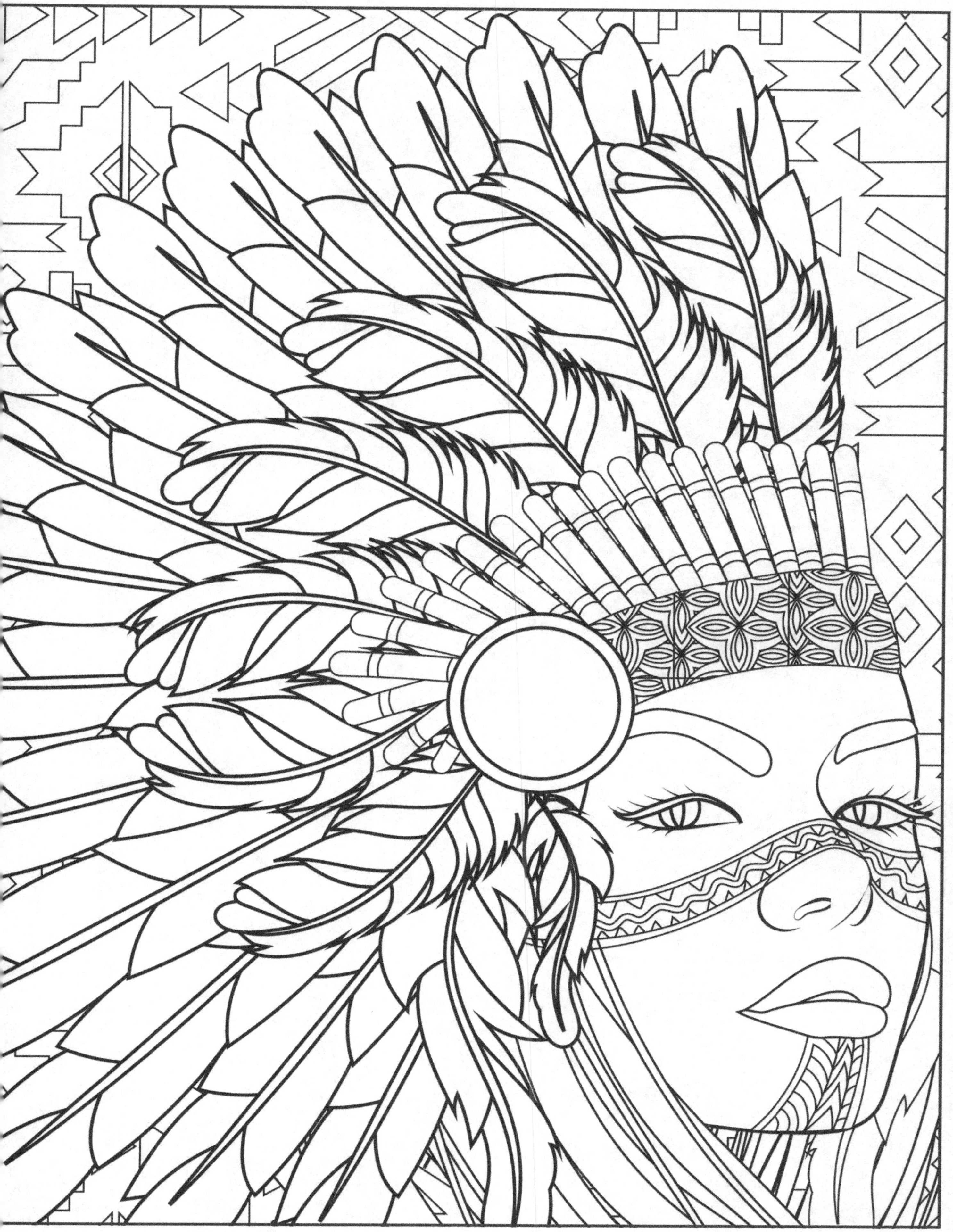

I AM
RELEASING
NEGATIVE
ENERGY AND
ATTRACTING
SERENITY.

✳ RELAXING THERAPY COLORING ✳

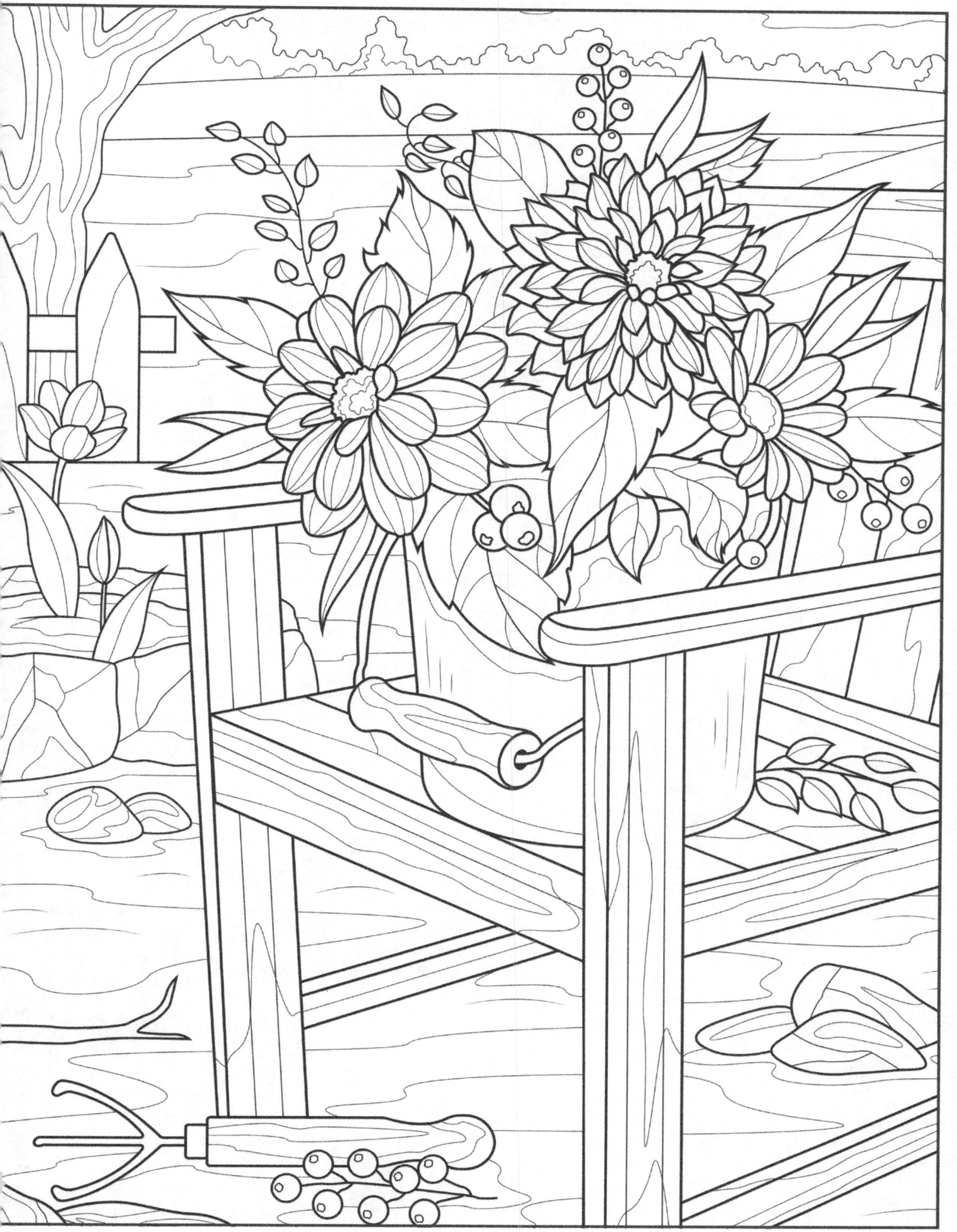

I AM
TRANQUIL,
RELAXED,
AND
AT EASE.

✶ RELAXING THERAPY COLORING ✶

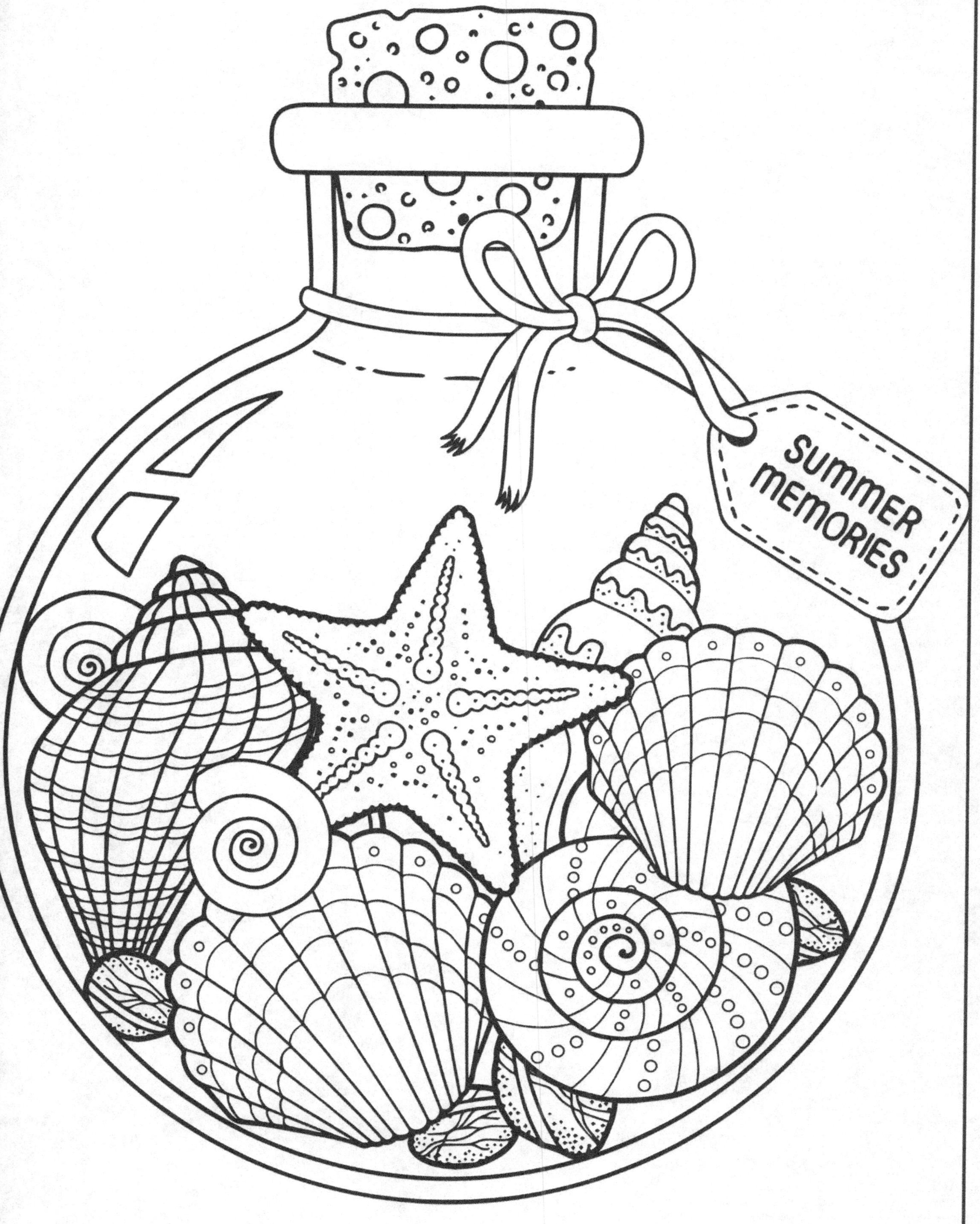
SUMMER
MEMORIES

I AM
IN HARMONY
WITH THE
RHYTHM OF
LIFE.

★ RELAXING THERAPY COLORING ★

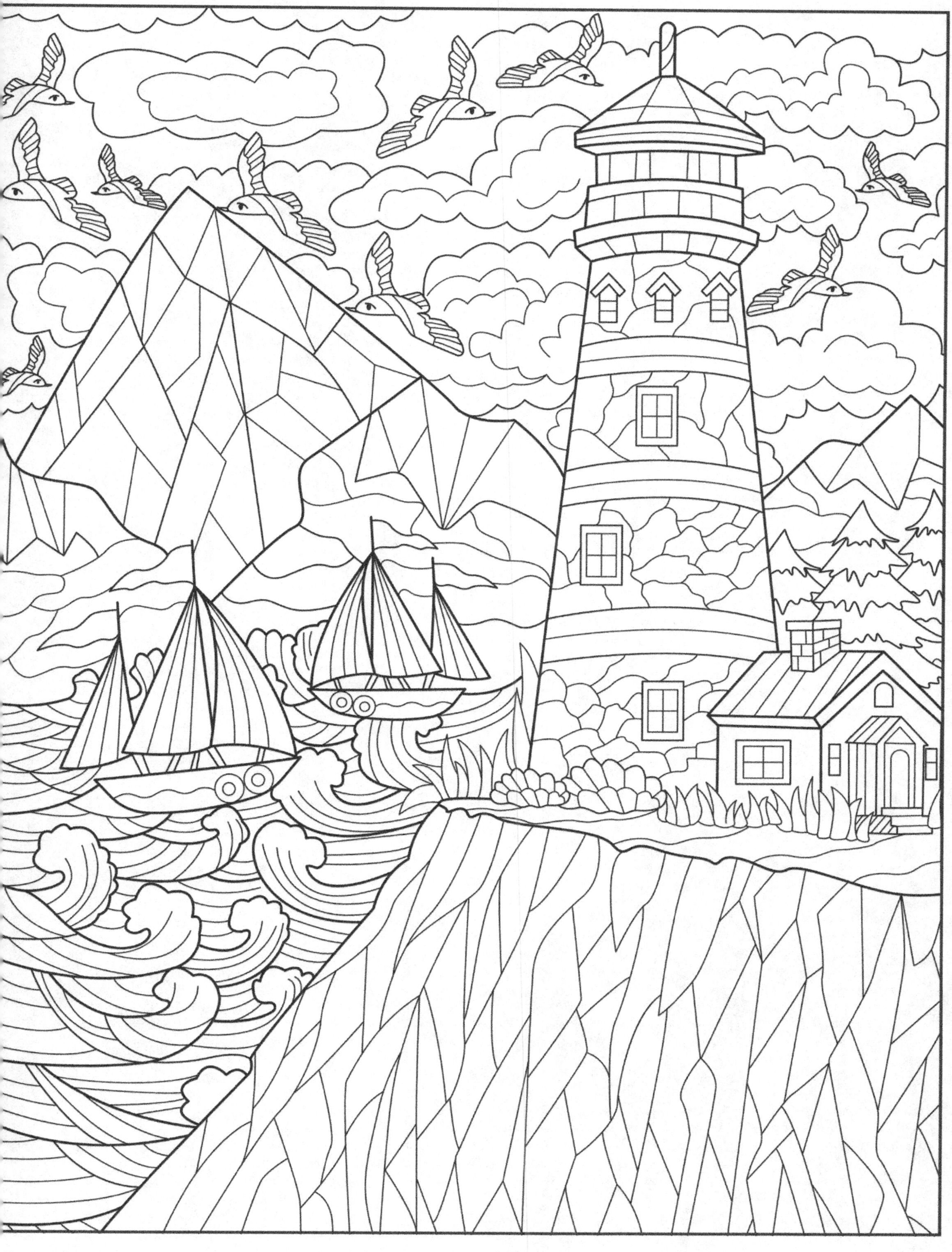

I AM ACCEPTING PEACE INTO EVERY ASPECT OF MY LIFE.

RELAXING THERAPY COLORING

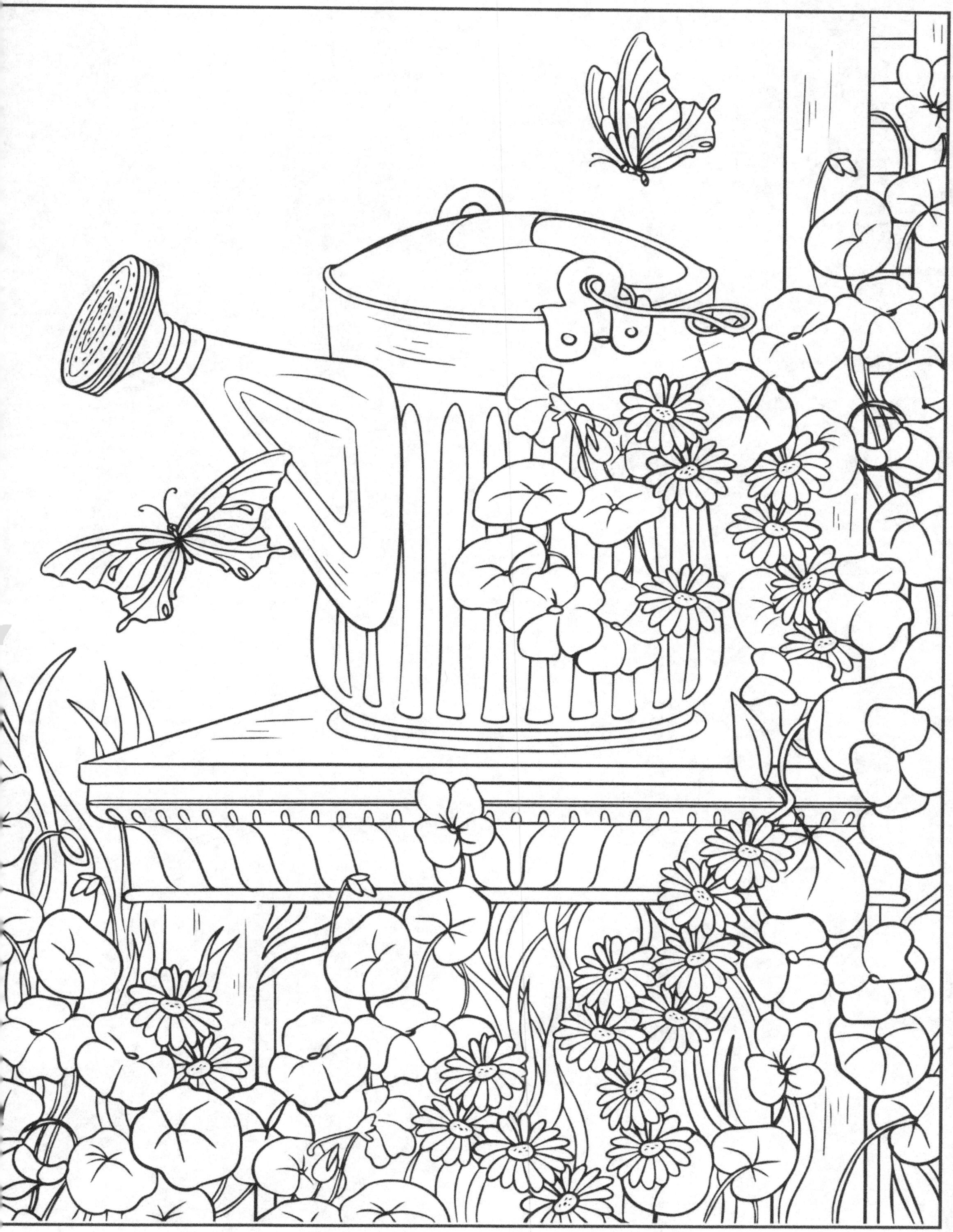

I AM
ROOTED IN
TRANQUILITY
AND
FLOURISHING
IN PEACE.

✷ RELAXING THERAPY COLORING ✷

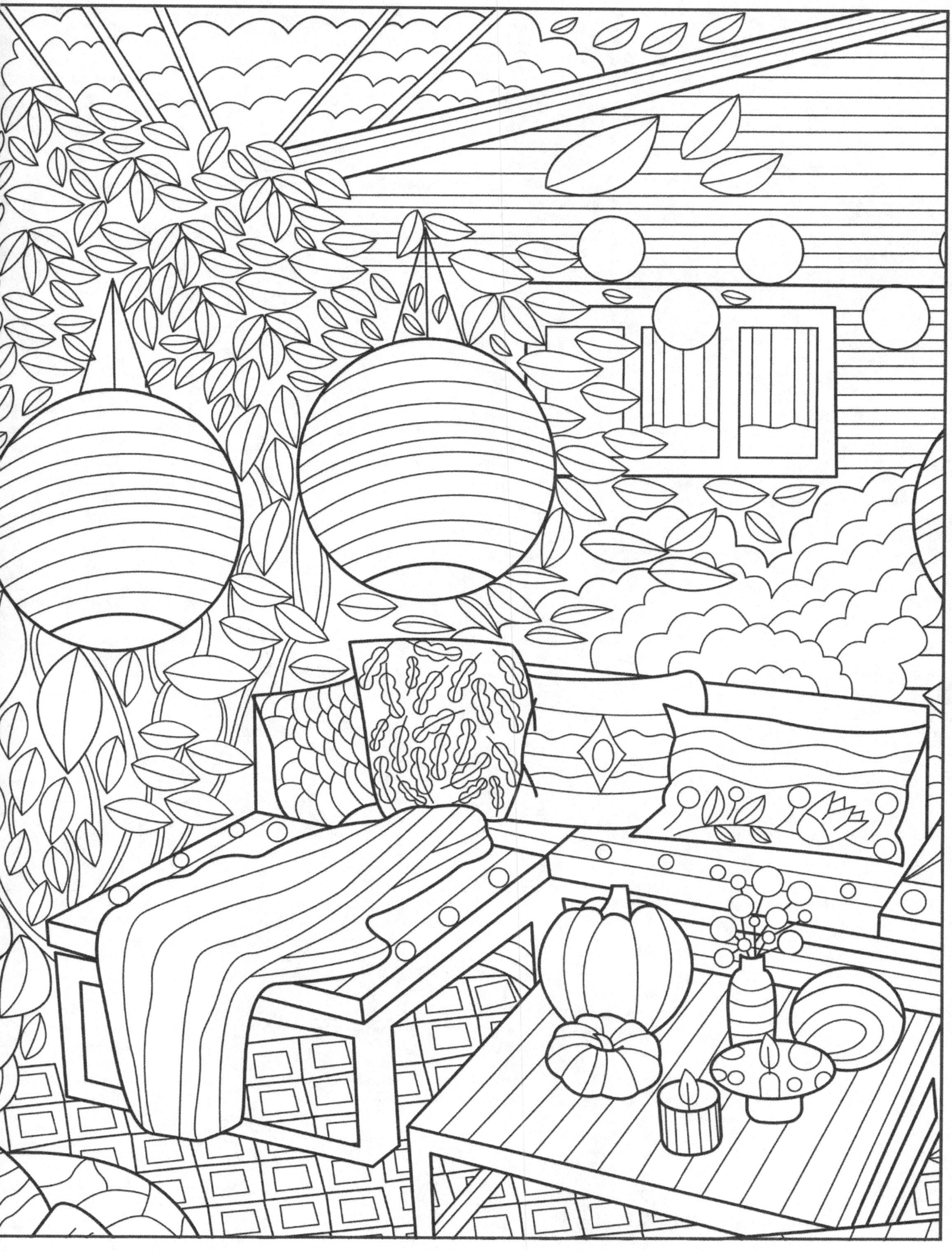

I AM SERENE, COMPOSED, AND CENTERED.

RELAXING THERAPY COLORING

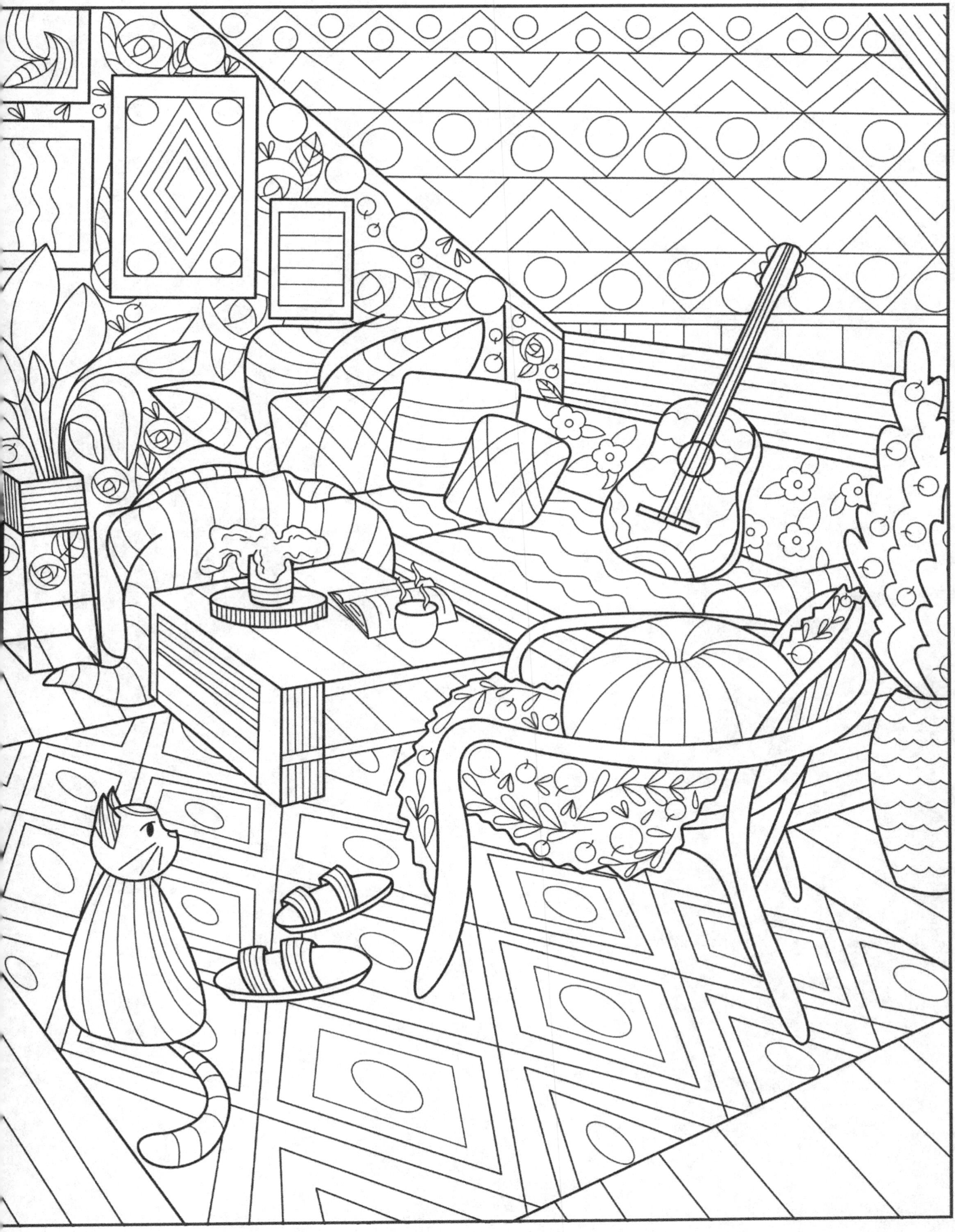

I AM BASKING IN THE GLOW OF PEACEFUL ENERGY.

RELAXING THERAPY COLORING

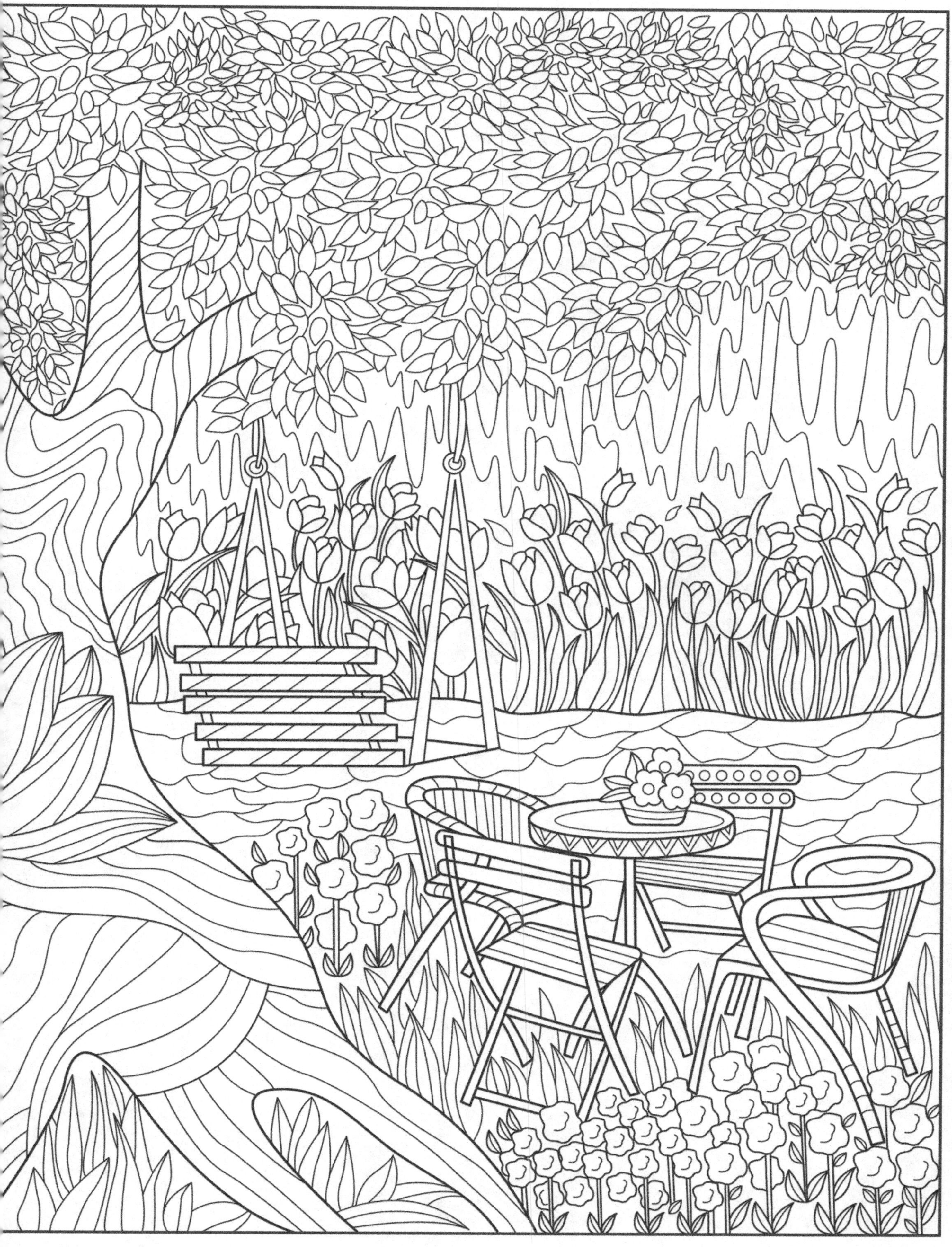

I AM CHOOSING CALM OVER CHAOS.

✴ RELAXING THERAPY COLORING ✴

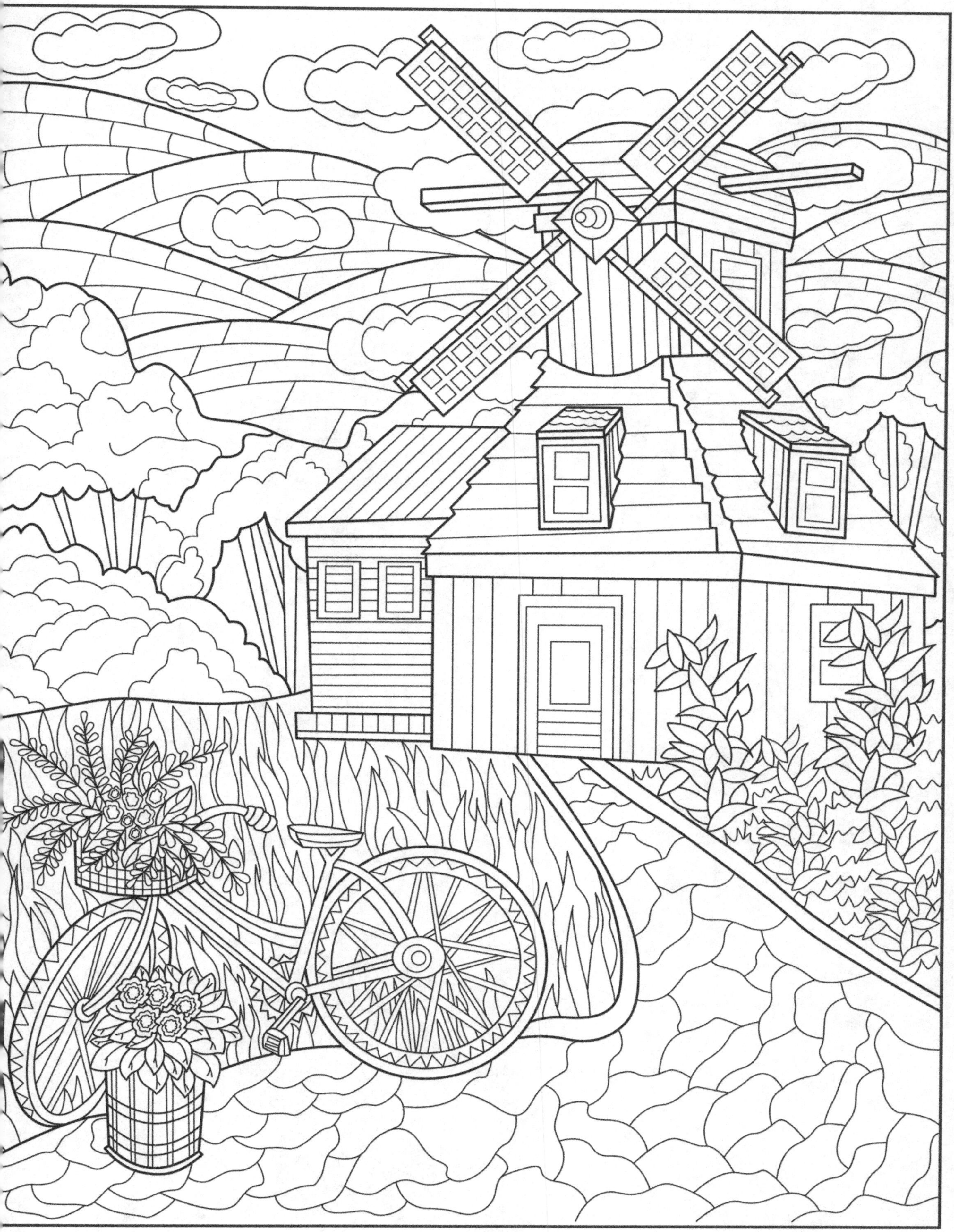

I AM
THE
ARCHITECT
OF MY
TRANQUILITY.

✴ RELAXING THERAPY COLORING ✴

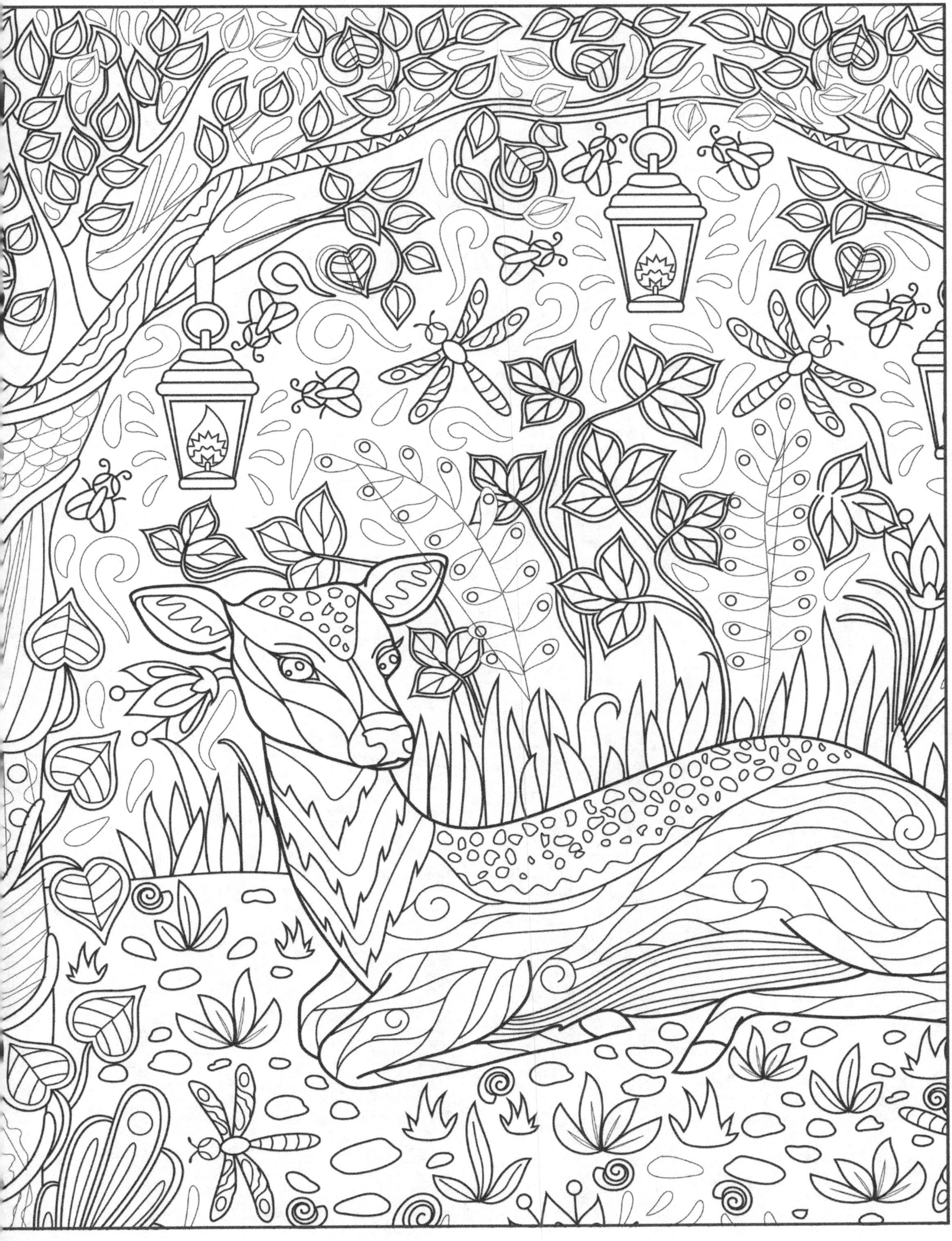

I AM
IN CONTROL
OF MY STRESS
LEVELS.

* RELAXING THERAPY COLORING *

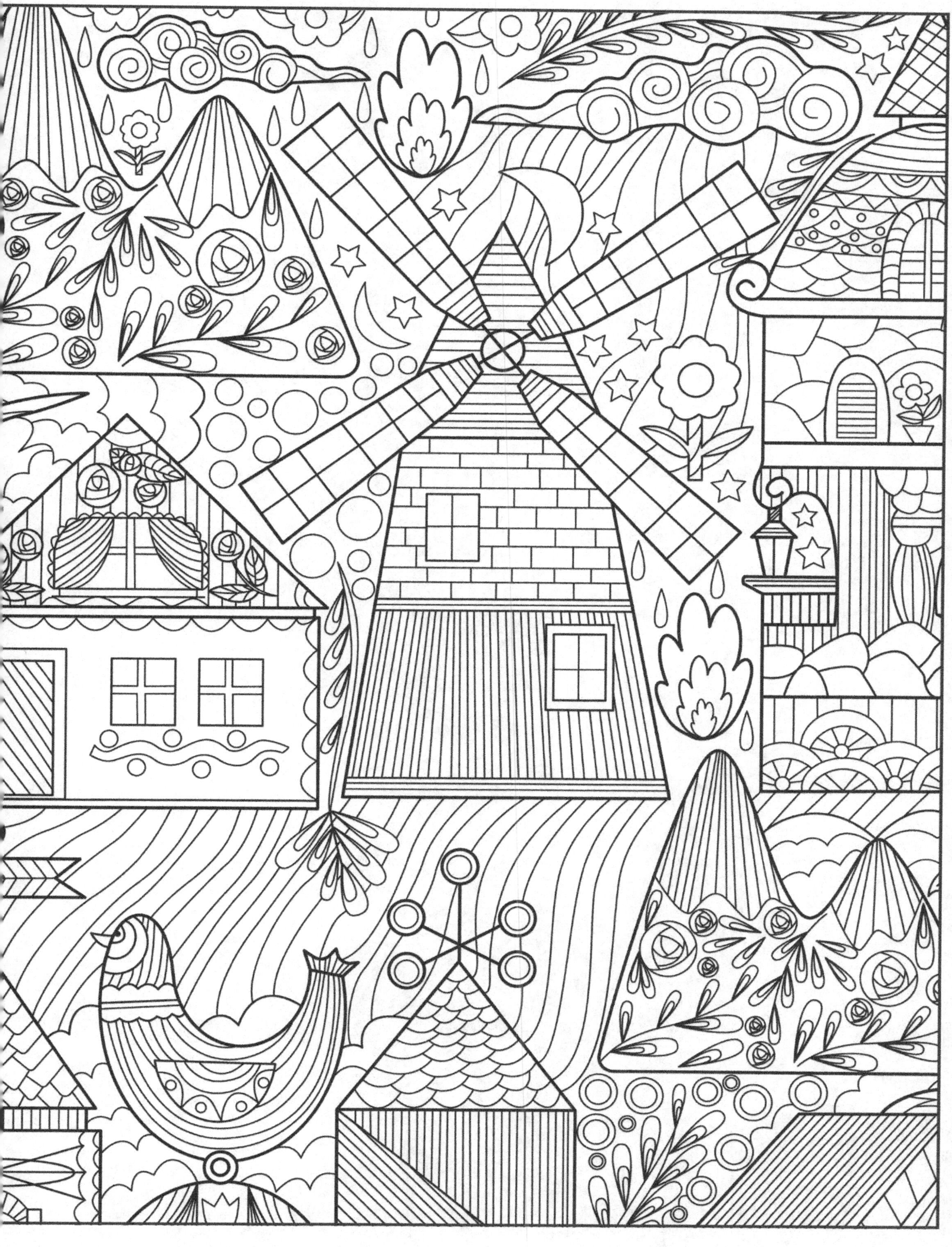

I AM FLOATING ON THE RIVER OF RELAXATION.

✷ RELAXING THERAPY COLORING ✷

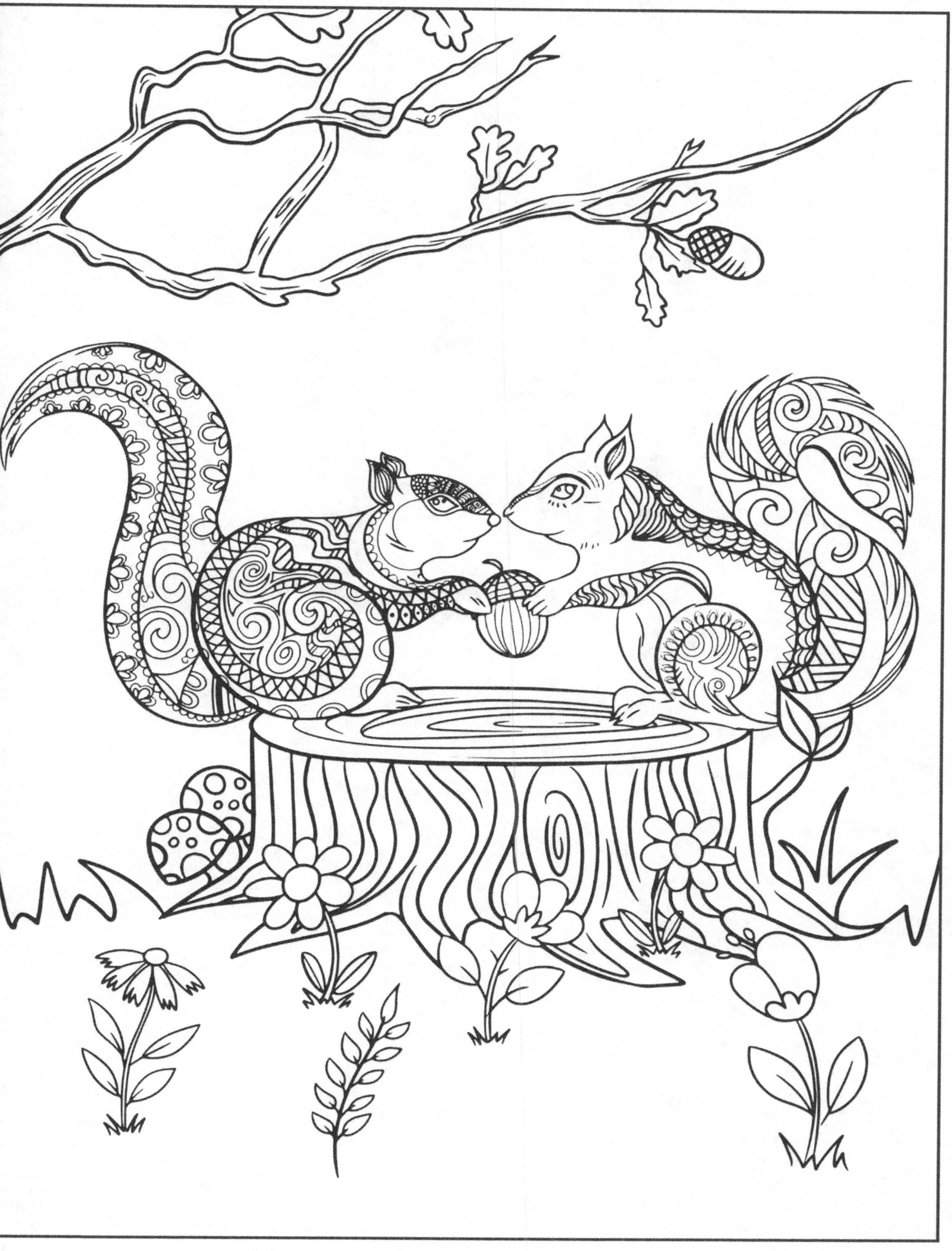

MY AURA
IS FILLED
WITH
CALMING
ENERGY.

RELAXING THERAPY COLORING

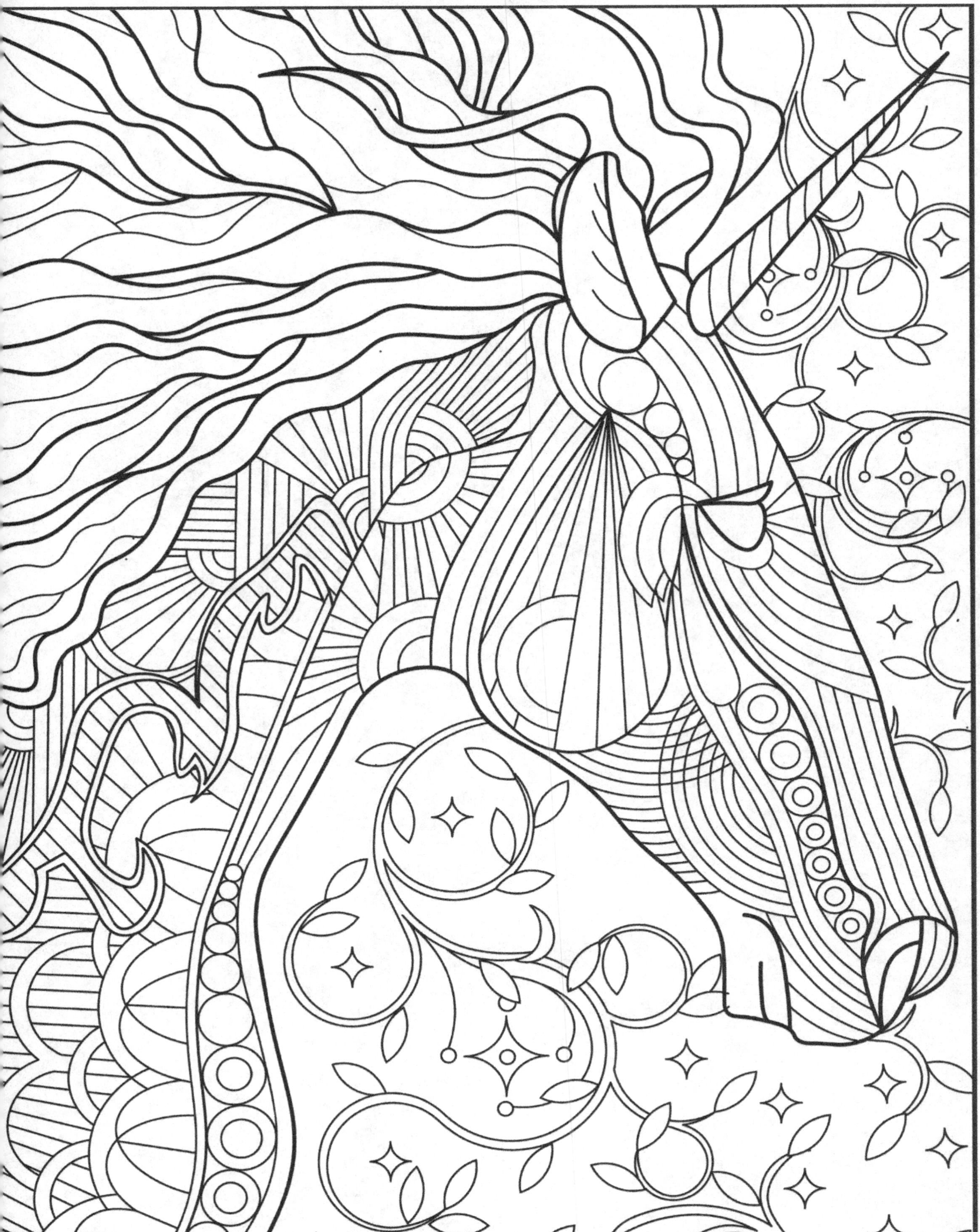

I AM TRANSFORMING ANXIETY INTO TRANQUILITY.

✷ RELAXING THERAPY COLORING ✷

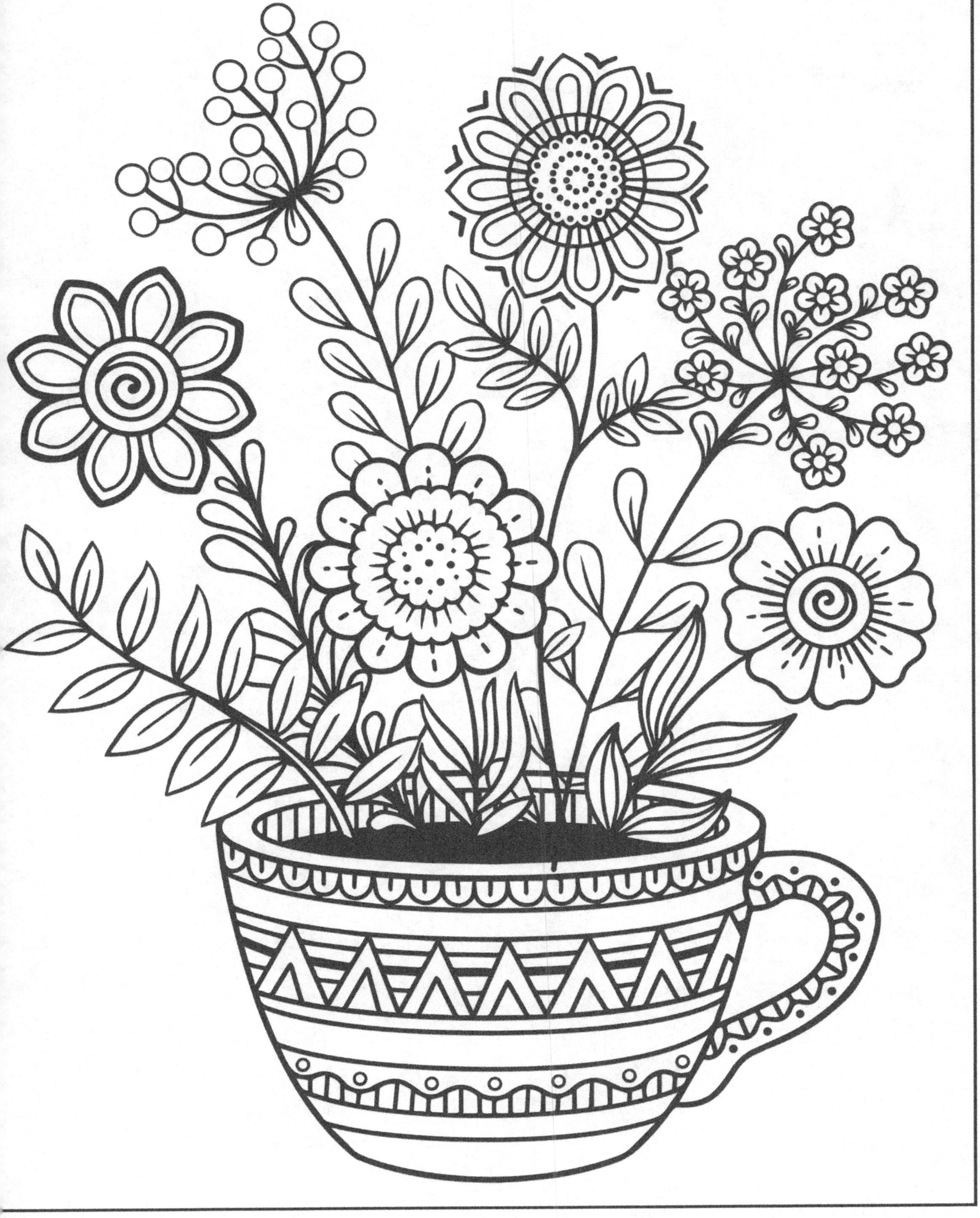

MY
THOUGHTS
ARE CALM,
MY SPIRIT
IS PEACEFUL.

RELAXING THERAPY COLORING

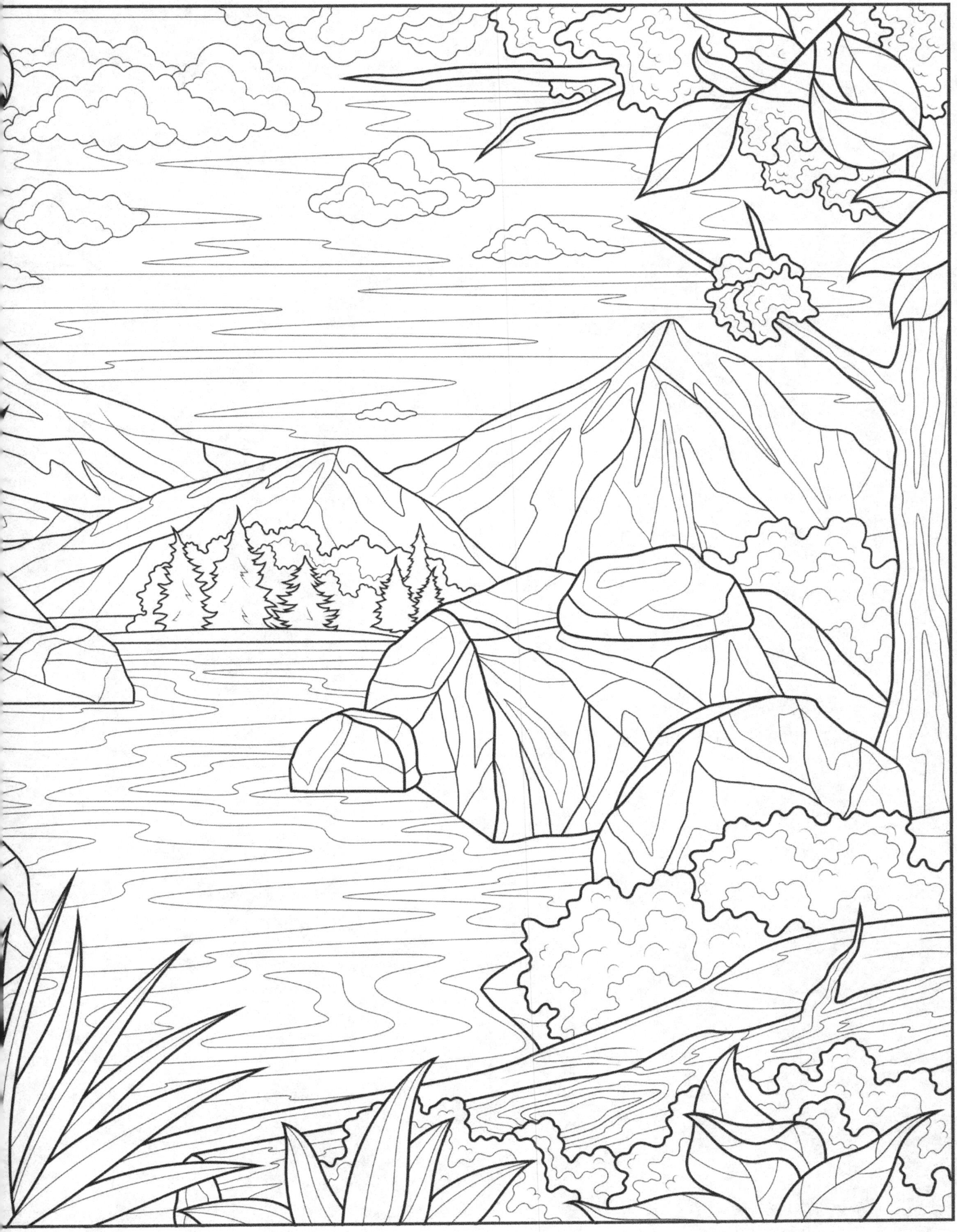

I AM BREATHING IN SERENITY AND BREATHING OUT STRESS.

* RELAXING THERAPY COLORING *

I AM SOAKING UP TRANQUILITY LIKE SUNSHINE.

✷ RELAXING THERAPY COLORING ✷

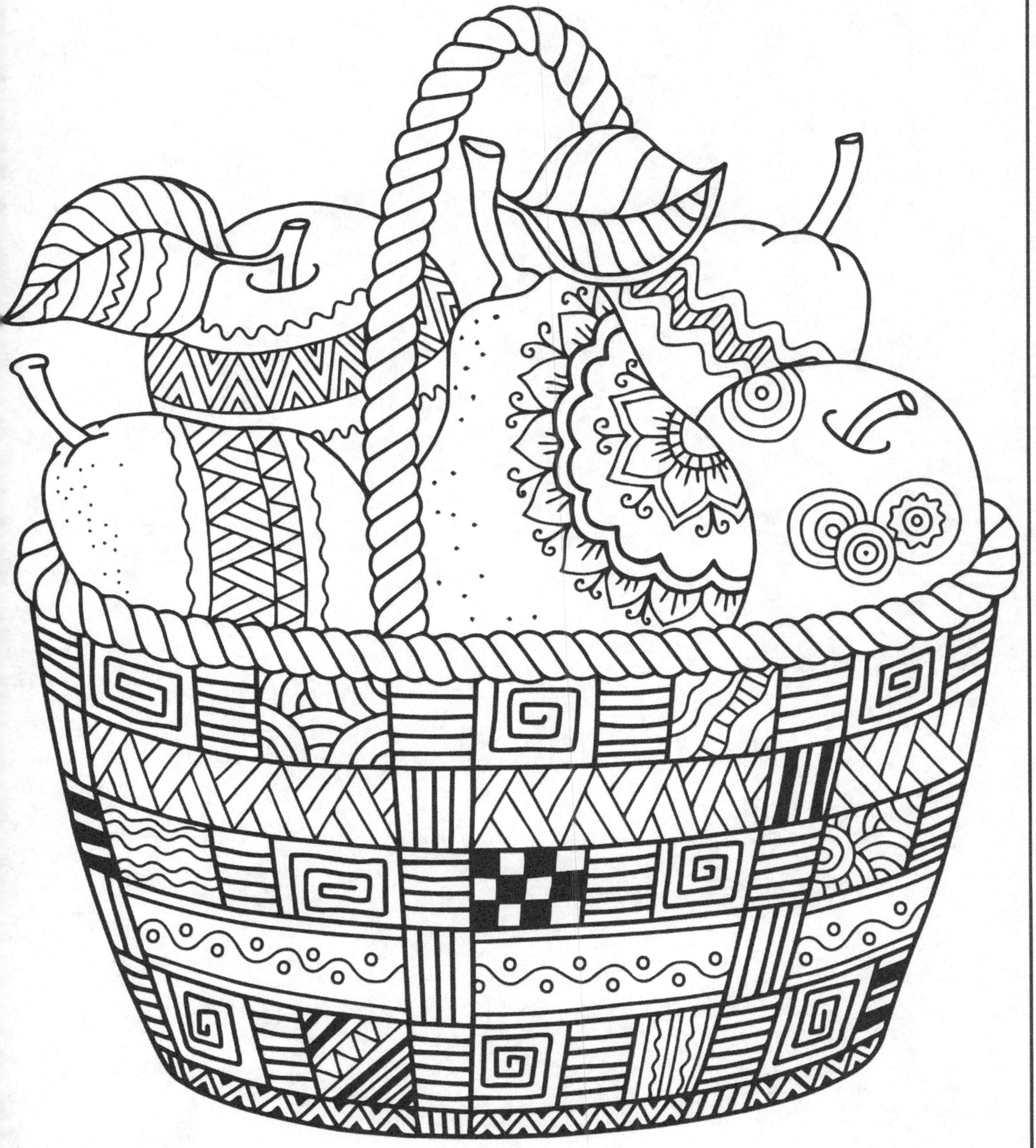

PEACE AND RELAXATION ARE BECOMING MY NATURAL STATES.

✶ RELAXING THERAPY COLORING ✶

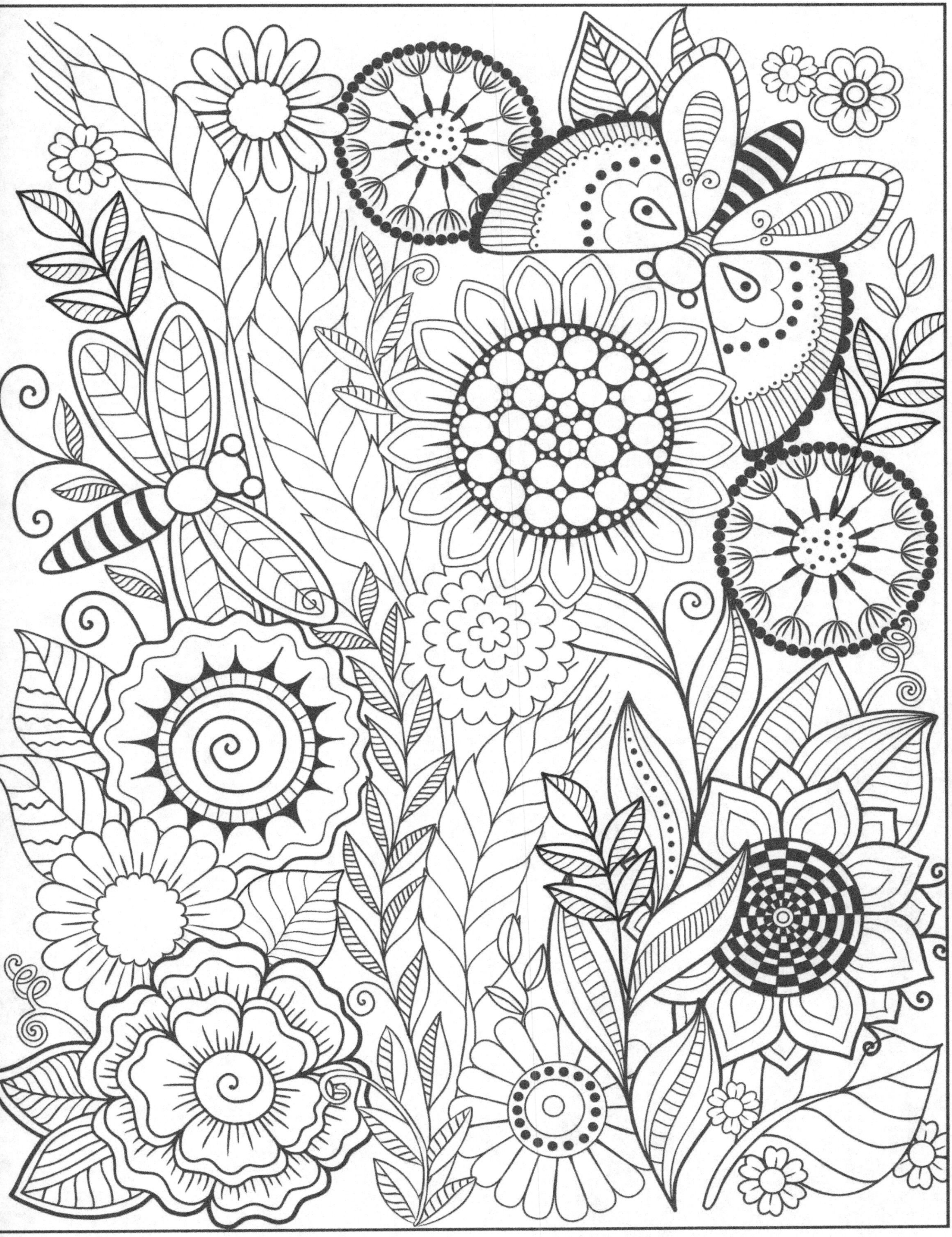

I AM CULTIVATING A GARDEN OF PEACE WITHIN ME.

✶ RELAXING THERAPY COLORING ✶

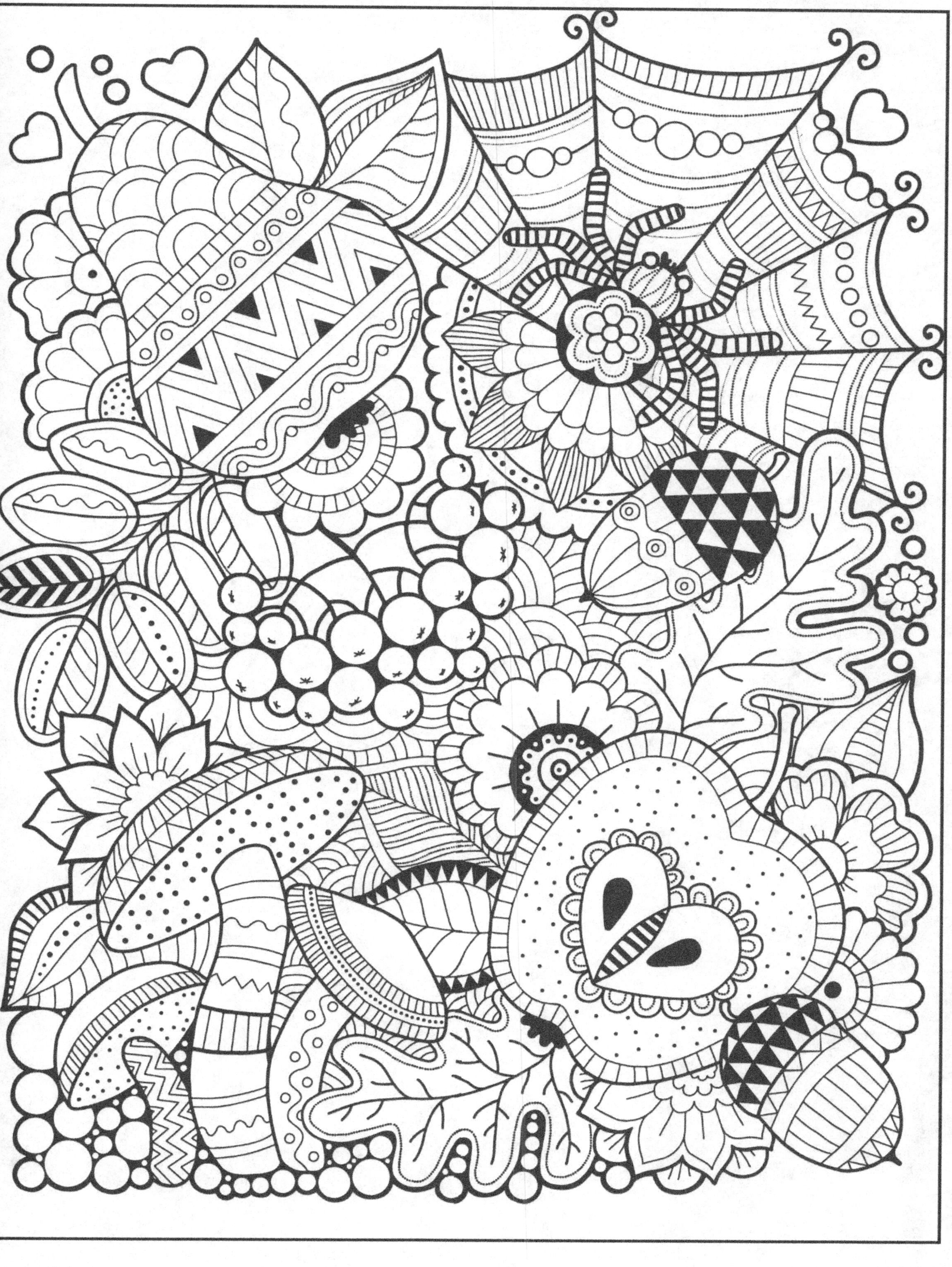

I AM TRANQUIL IN MIND, RELAXED IN BODY.

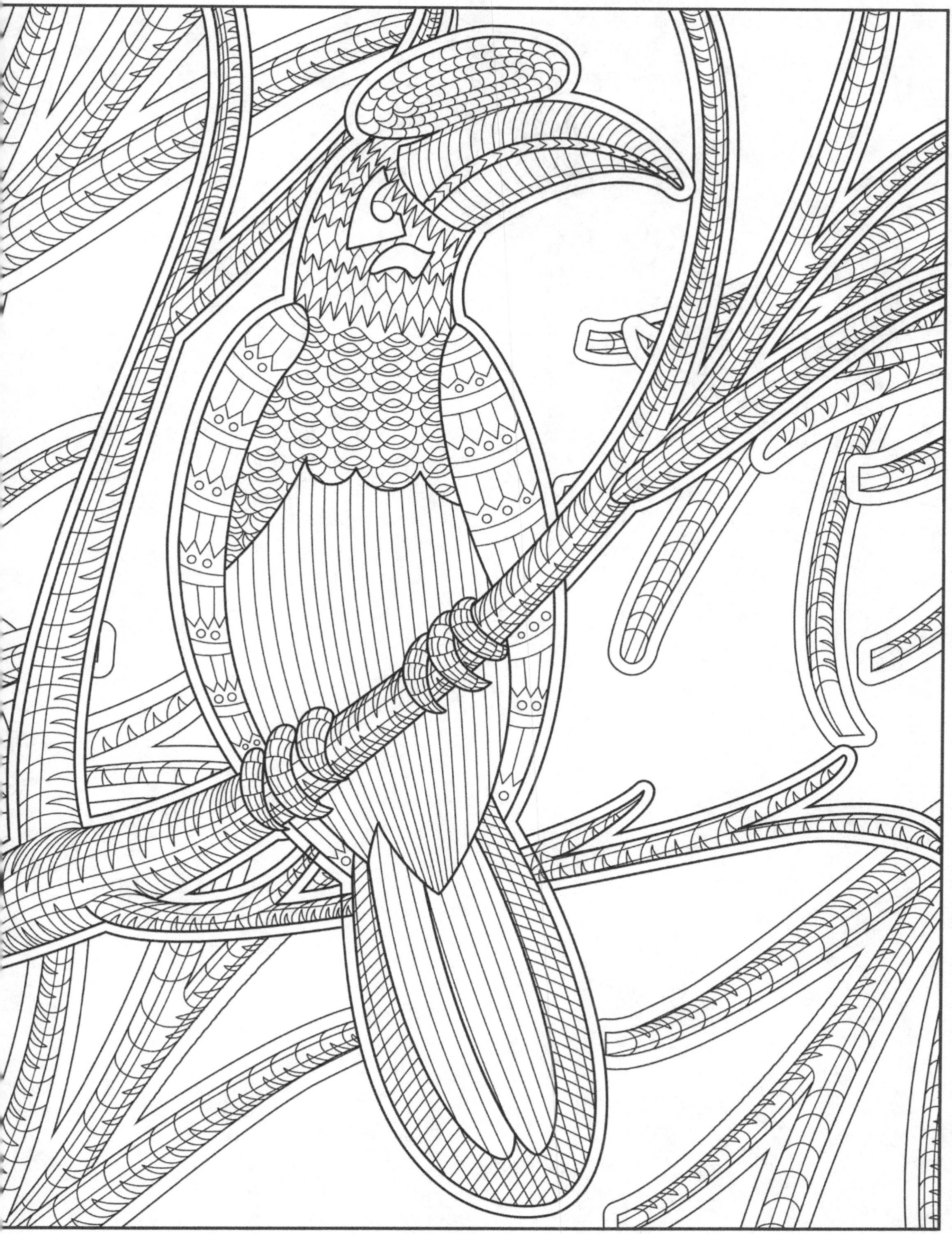

EVERY DAY, IN
EVERY WAY, I
AM
BECOMING
MORE
RELAXED.

RELAXING THERAPY COLORING

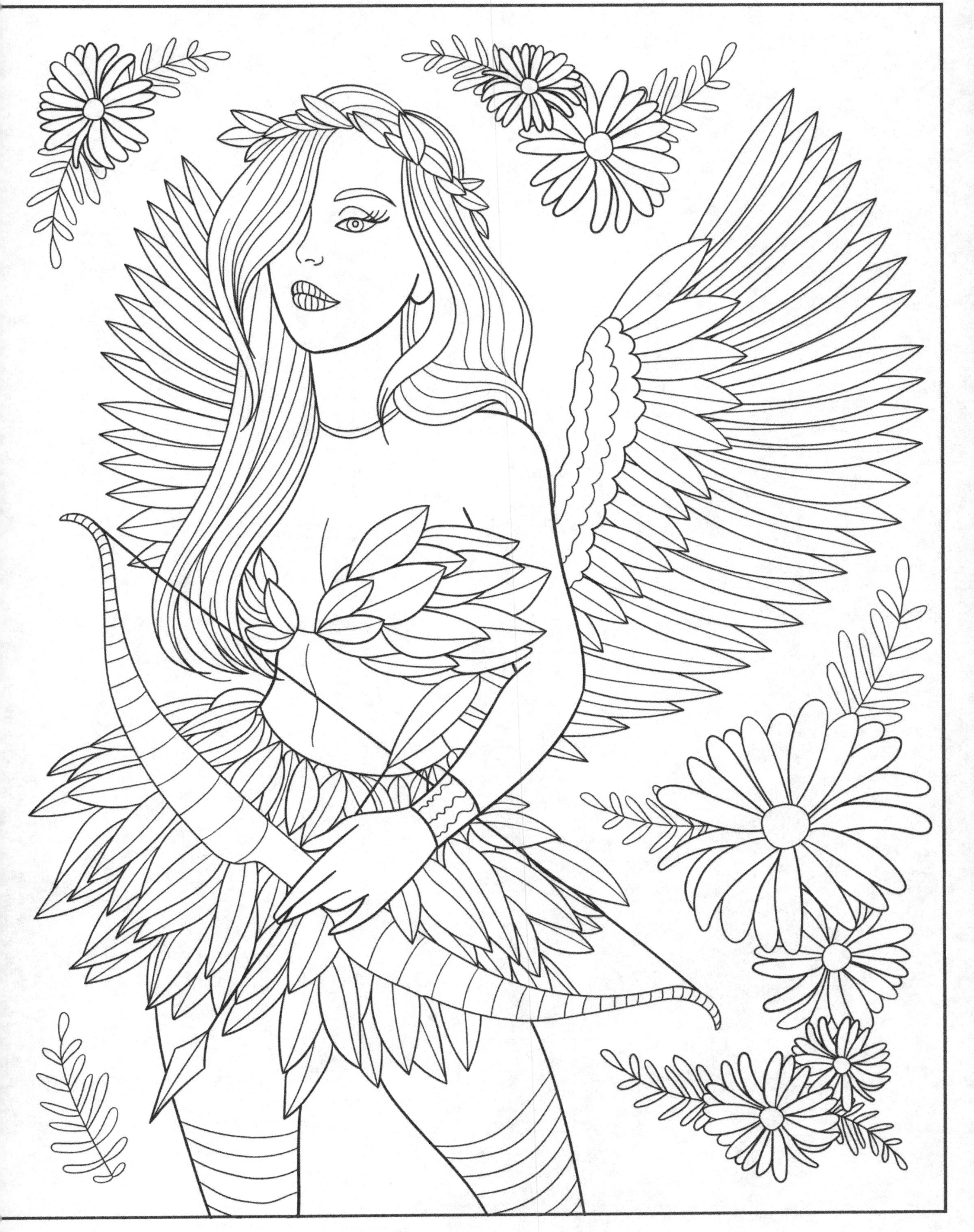

I AM
A
SANCTUARY
OF PEACE.

✳ RELAXING THERAPY COLORING ✳

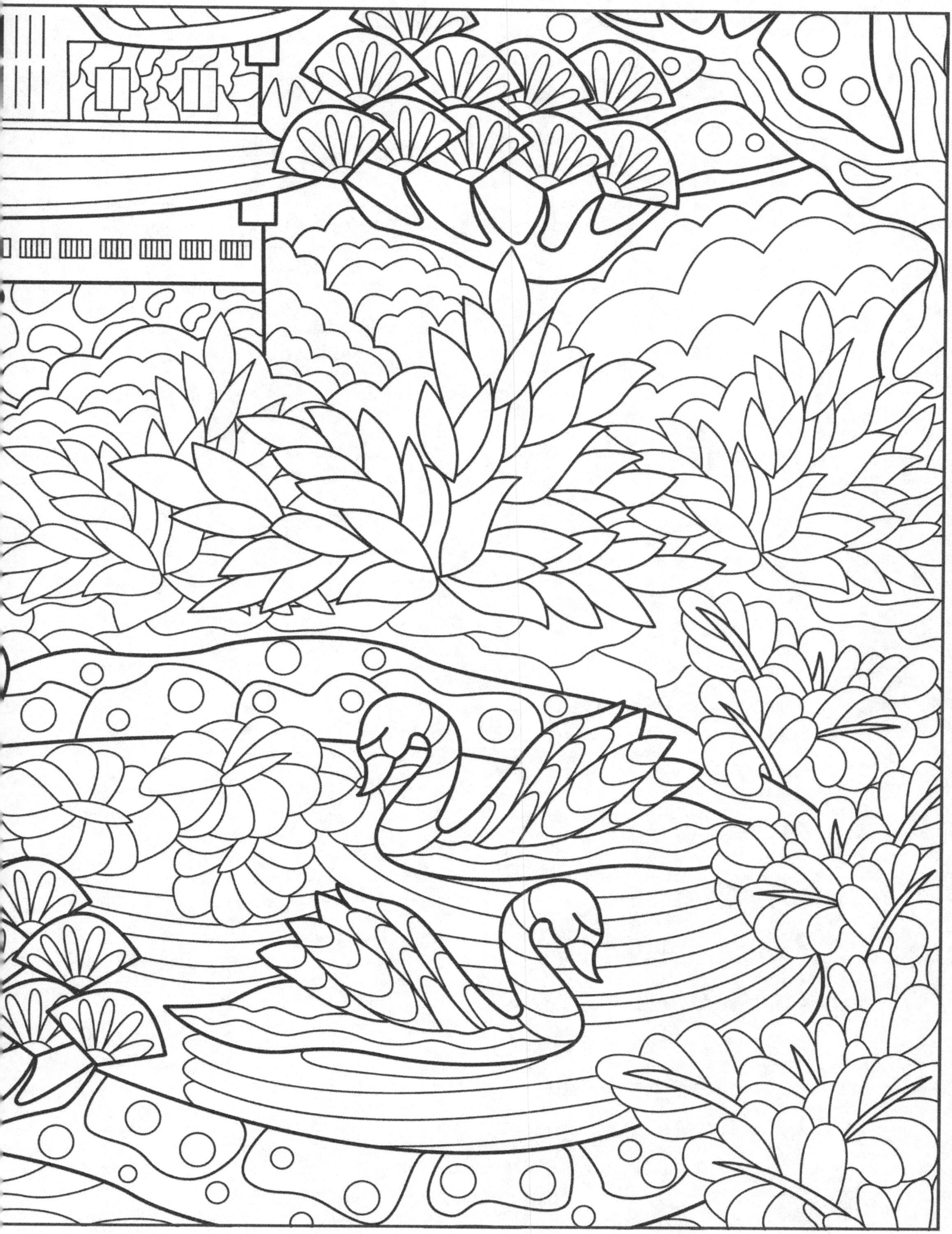

I AM EMBRACING CALMNESS IN EVERY MOMENT.

✳ RELAXING THERAPY COLORING ✳

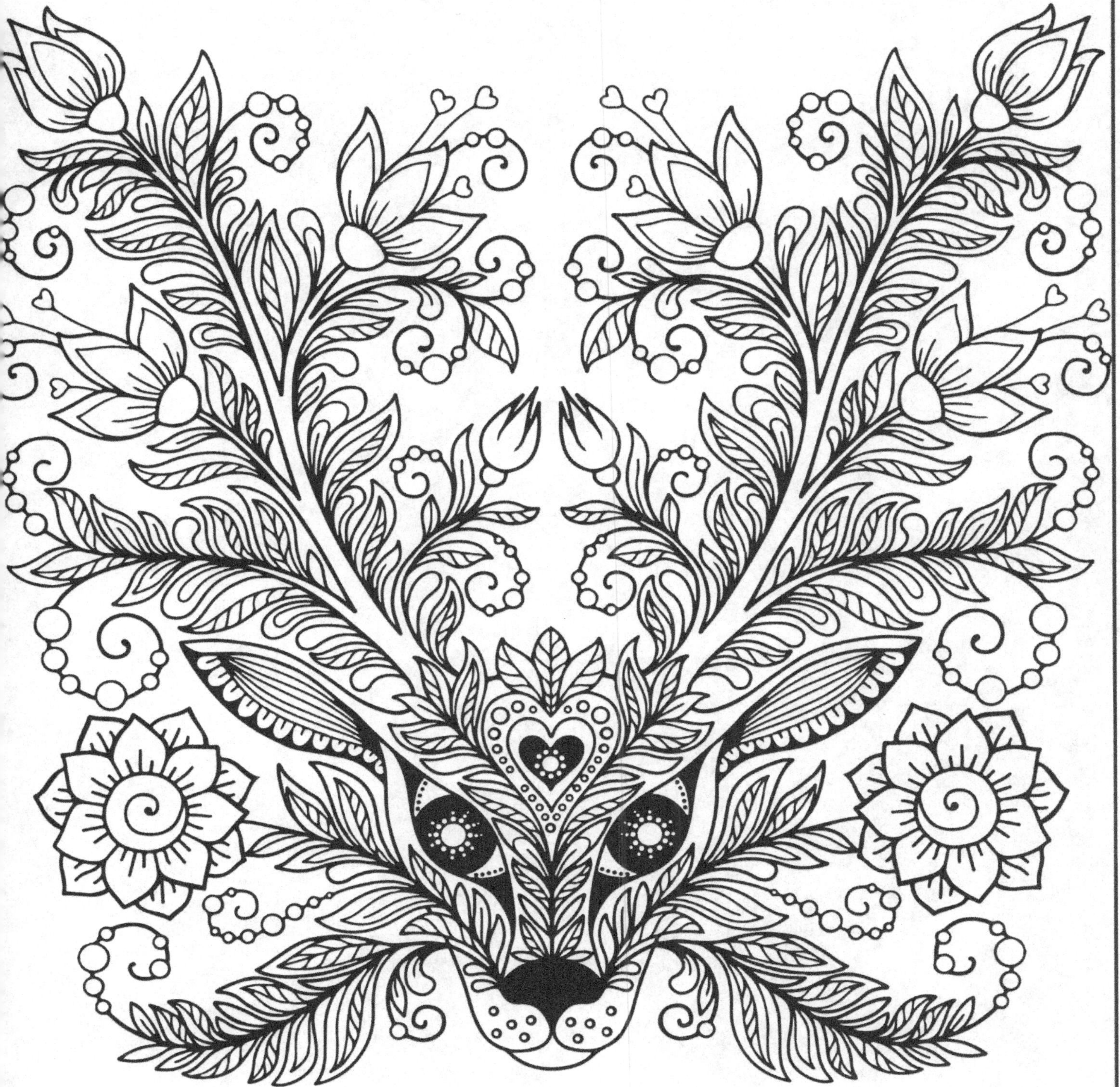

I AM
THE
EMBODIMENT
OF
TRANQUILITY.

RELAXING THERAPY COLORING

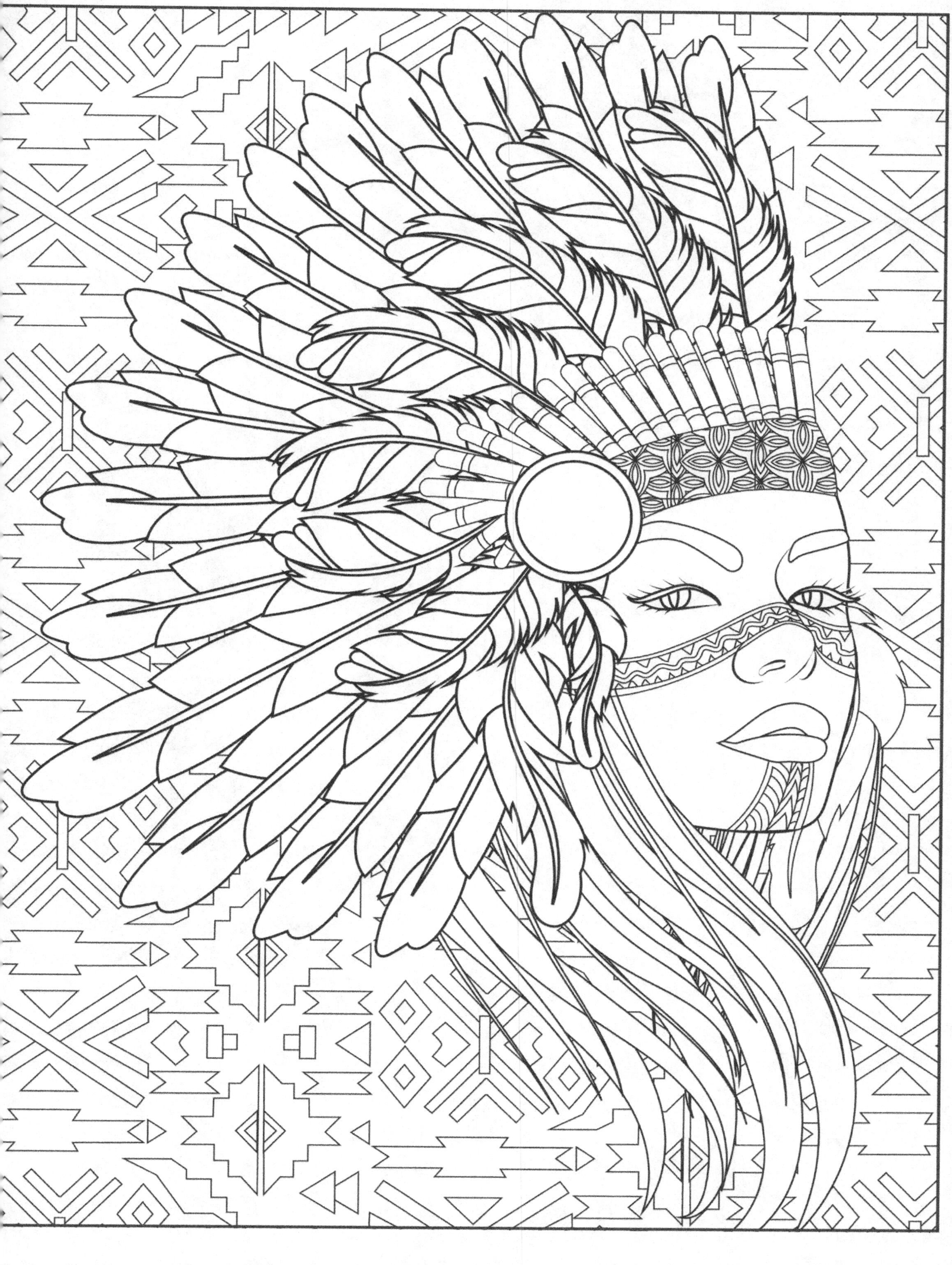

I AM FILLED WITH THE SOOTHING RHYTHM OF RELAXATION.

✴ RELAXING THERAPY COLORING ✴

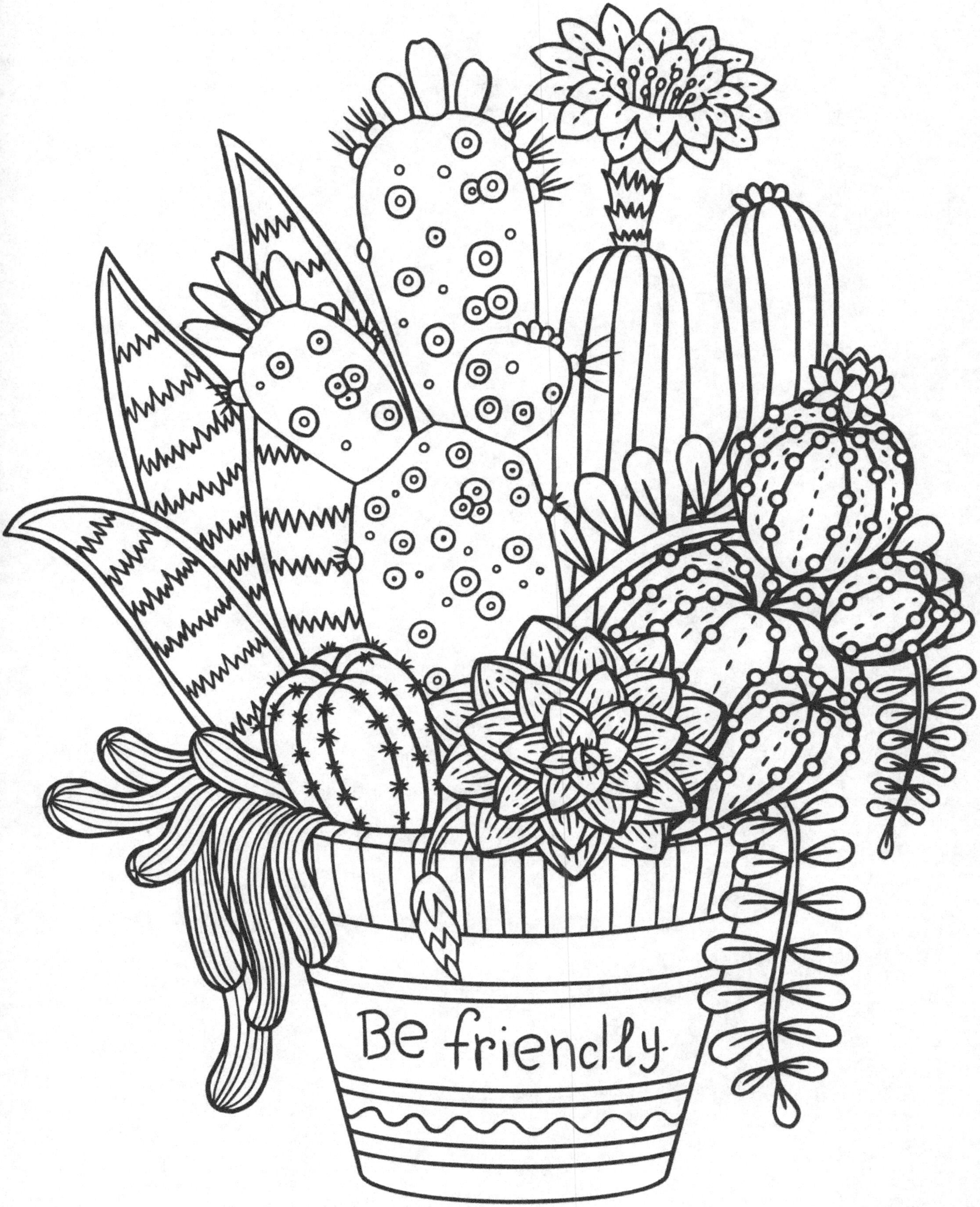
Be friendly.

SCAN ME!
TO GET FREE COLORING PAGES

Unwind with our free Unique Coloring pages every other Friday. Enjoy a one-of-a-kind coloring experience with intricate designs and bold lines. Sign up now for a fun and relaxing hobby that brings joy and stress relief.

FREE COLORING PAGES

PRINT Unlimited Copies Anytime You Want --- NO LIMIT
Creative and Unique Designs You Can't Find Anywhere!

For Inquiries Write to info@therapycoloring.com

Made in United States
Orlando, FL
01 September 2023